Psychic Children

Understanding their Psychic Gifts
Amazing True Stories of
Children's Psychic Gifts

Psychic Children

Understanding their Psychic Gifts
Amazing True Stories of
Children's Psychic Gifts

Joanne Brocas

Author of *Feel the Vibes*

A Psychic & Spiritual Development Book

BOOKS

Winchester, UK
Washington, USA

First published by O-Books, 2010
O-Books is an imprint of John Hunt Publishing Ltd., The Bothy, Deershot Lodge, Park Lane, Ropley,
Hants, SO24 0BE, UK
office1@o-books.net
www.o-books.com

For distributor details and how to order please visit the 'Ordering' section on our website.

Text copyright: Joanne Brocas 2009

ISBN: 978 1 84694 367 6

A CIP catalogue record for this book is available from the British Library.

Design: Stuart Davies

Printed in the UK by CPI Antony Rowe
Printed in the USA by Offset Paperback Mfrs, Inc

We operate a distinctive and ethical publishing philosophy in all
areas of our business, from our global network of authors to
production and worldwide distribution.

CONTENTS

3: Children & Angels

4: Intuitive Children

5: Children's Past Lives

Acknowledgements

To my husband Jock, who is my soulmate and best friend

I dedicate this book to my parents,
My mother Glenys, her strength and independence have helped
me to follow my heart
To my father William, his sense of humour has given me a
light- hearted spark
I would also like to acknowledge the following people,
My nephew Liam
My brother Jamie & Sister- in- Law Jan
My friend Sheila Colaluca who has encouraged me in writing
this book
Finally my gratitude is for John Hunt, my publisher at
O-Books. I am truly grateful for giving me the opportunity to
get my books out there. John, you are amazing and I will never
forget what you have done for me. I also want to thank Trevor
and the staff at O-Books for their support.

Introduction

Psychic children can see what others cannot. They have remarkable psychic gifts that enable them to tap into the spirit world and receive information that to most adults is unobtainable. This fascinating book will help you as a parent of a psychic child to fully understand what it is your child is experiencing. You will also read other real life stories of psychic children including the author's own psychic childhood. This book will help you to discover ways to enhance your child's natural psychic side to flourish and grow in a gentle, safe and guided manner without any fear or control. It can also help you to discover your psychic side if you have grown up with a fascination of all things psychic.

In reading this book, you will discover the wonderful array of psychic gifts and abilities that children possess. Things like having imaginary friends, talking to spirit people and seeing angels. Maybe your child tells you things that they could not possibly have known; information that predicts the future or even things that reveals the past. Does your child talk about their life before they were born, either somewhere else on earth – within another family or when they were at home in the spirit world? If so then read on, as this is the book for you. You will read real life stories of children's past lives, some children have even been known to have drawn or painted pictures of when they were at home in Heaven. The information and stories within this book will help to broaden your awareness of psychic children.

Children are amazingly sensitive and use their feelings to guide them long before they begin to talk, they have an innate sense of good and bad or to put it another way, they can feel if someone is a good seed or a bad apple. This is their inbuilt protection called 'intuition' that if gently encouraged will lovingly assist them throughout the rest of their lives. This book will also help you to understand your own intuitive nature giving you the clues and nudges within its pages to remember and enhance your own natural psychic side. Do you need any help and guidance with how to handle a psychic child? Are you worried about any unusual or alarming occurrences affecting your child and your home? There is a chapter on ghosts and earthbound spirits who visit psychic children which can sometimes cause them to be fearful. Information in this chapter will leave you with a clear picture of the correct action you need to take and the issues needed to be addressed to make things right.

In reading this book, you will understand how to develop a deeper connection to your child. Psychic children are extra sensitive and this sensitivity can reveal itself in a multitude of ways with side effects such as sleep problems, being fearful of the dark, fussy eating and tantrums. You will also see the creativity and light that shines from within the child when they do the things that make them feel wonderful inside. Each child is unique with individual gifts and talents each expressed in different ways. Encouragement of their creativity will help to inspire them to create success and harmony in their futures. Gentle exercises are included in this book to help guide you and your child in enhancing your sixth sense.

This book will provide you with the solace and the solutions that are needed to help you totally understand your psychic child and will enable you to connect the dots and realise how to best help your child along their destiny. If you have a child who displays any of what you have read, then this is the book for you. Look no further as you delve into the life and experience of a psychic child, for remember you were once a child too and this book will also help you to understand yourself.

Joanne Brocas

Chapter One

Psychic Kids

'The most beautiful thing we can experience is the mysterious. It is the source of all true art and all science'
Albert Einstein

Everyone is Psychic

Everybody is psychic to varying degrees and children especially so. You will soon read about real life stories of children's psychic experiences that may even jog your own memory of such things happening to you when you were small. What you read can help you to simplify and understand more about these natural psychic abilities which can then put your mind at ease. Sometimes not knowing what is going on with your child or yourself can cause stress, fear and a need for answers. I hope that you will receive such answers here to help you with the support you may need at this time in your life.

Each chapter will bring you a new inner awareness of the sixth sense and some will include practical exercises to help bring healing and harmony to both you and your child. Learning how to use and control their natural psychic ability within their lives has the potential to clearly help your child create the life of their dreams and desires. I will show you ways in which to keep your child's psychic gifts in balance so that they do not become overwhelmed or frightened. Some children will use their psychic gifts without a care in the world while others may be scared or nervous as they do not understand what is happening. This can make you worried but as you learn more about your psychic child you will discover the ways in which to help them.

Children's Psychic Gifts

There are many different psychic gifts that children possess and some of the more well known ones include seeing and talking with imaginary friends, spirit people and angels. Other psychic gifts include children using their sixth sense and intuition to give psychic guidance to grown- ups or to reassure them on a worrying matter. You will read some stories about this in the chapter called the intuitive child. Some children are able to give future predictions of situations or events that have not yet happened. Other children will receive telepathic information that can be transferred from mind to mind and they can even read their mothers' thoughts. Telepathic information can also be transferred from spirits or imaginary friends and the child would then have the ability of mediumship. Sometimes a child can receive information that will just pop into their minds and they seem to *just know* something without knowing why they know it. Emma *just knew* that her Grandmother was coming over to visit, even though her family thought she was on holiday in Italy; more about this in a later chapter.

Sometimes children will reveal events of the past even though the child would have had no prior knowledge about the event. It would have happened before they were born or it was unknown to them. Other psychic children will talk about their past lives within different families and have specific memories and information that they could not possibly have discovered from their current life, just as Harry did when he remembered being in the war. You will read about his story in the chapter on children's past lives.

Then you have the children who remember being at home in the spirit realms before they were even born. And the children who have experienced NDE's known as near death experiences and have painted or drawn pictures of what it was like in Heaven. All children are born psychic as they have recently left the other side and are still in tune with the spirit world's vibration. Adults who have lost touch with their natural psychic side have literally forgotten their own spiritual potential of who they really are. It is never too late to remember the truth of who you really are or where you came from. Realising this truth will help you to kick- start your intuition and psychic senses to come back into your conscious awareness and daily life. The sixth sense comes with a full array of psychic abilities; read on to see if you notice any of these abilities expressed by you or your child.

The Psychic Abilities of Clairsentience & Intuition

Clairsentience is the gift of sensing and feeling energy vibrations from people, spirits, places and objects and then interpreting those feelings to receive accurate information. It is closely connected to intuitive feelings although with the intuition you can also receive intuitive thoughts that are inspirational or revealing. Intuitive thoughts can help you by providing the answer to a question you have been wondering about or by suddenly revealing the insight that you may need to solve a problem. As a medium I sometimes find myself using clairsentience to feel how the spirit died. If the spirit had a cancer condition I may suddenly and momentarily feel quite sick. This goes immediately on mentioning the cancer condition.

When my students have used the gift of clairsentience to perform psychic readings, they have felt aches and pains appear on them in the same place as the person having the reading has them. Once they mention these aches and pains to the person having the reading then they disappear as quickly as they came. Psychic children who are strong in the gift of clairsentience will show signs of being extra sensitive to others feelings. They will be compassionate and caring but they can also be worriers and sometimes be quite anxious. They would worry about the safety of their loved ones and may at times become quite clingy with them. They may also be fearful of the dark and have problems

5

sleeping as their sensitive side can manifest nightmares.

Clairsentient children will absorb the energy vibrations of others and this can sometimes make them feel unwell or irritable. The good thing about being clairsentient, though, is that it will help you to develop and strengthen your intuitive nature. You can then rely on the feedback of your feelings to help make wise decisions and choices within your life. Listening to the intuition can help to keep you safe from harm by alerting you to any imminent danger. A practical exercise to help strengthen the intuition is included in the chapter on the intuitive child along with ways in which to clear any absorbed foreign energies.

Note – *foreign energies belong to another source and are not part of your own auric field. This is what can make you feel out of sorts and off balance.*

The Psychic Abilities of Clairaudience, Telepathy & Mediumship

Clairaudience is the gift of inner hearing and obtaining information through sound vibrations that can be heard inside the mind. It is like when you speak to yourself with silent thoughts; say your name silently in your mind right now and you will know what I mean. Sometimes the thoughts will feel like they are your own as they sound like your own, this is normal or you may actually recognise that they belong to a voice that you know. Other times they will sound unfamiliar to you. You can also experience clairaudience by hearing words spoken out loud as if they are coming from the same room as you. This however is quite rare and most psychics will receive the information within their minds.

To hear spirit out loud is an amazing experience, I have been woken up by someone calling out my name although I did not recognise who it was. Mediums such as John Edward will use the gift of clairaudience to be able to communicate quickly with the spirit world, usually receiving the spirit's name. A medium is simply a channel or intermediary that is used by the spirit person to transmit their message, usually through telepathy and clairaudience so the medium can then pass it on to their loved ones on earth. You can also think of it in this way, the medium being the actual telephone that is needed to connect two people to be able to talk with each other over a distance.

Telepathy is the ability to send and receive thoughts from one person to another. Telepathy is quite common to experience and you have probably had instances yourself when you and someone else suddenly say the same thing at the same time. This can happen because you both picked up on each other's thoughts. My husband and I find ourselves doing this quite often. I have been out food shopping and I suddenly buy something that I had not planned to, only to find out that my husband was sending his thoughts out to me about what he wanted. This has happened so many times and it never ceases to amaze us. Telepathy can also happen when you are running a particular song through your head without singing it out loud and then you discover that the person with you starts singing the exact same song. Amazing or what?

Spirits also use the channel of telepathy to deliver information quickly to the medium and the medium can also ask questions back and wait for a response. Information can sometimes be transmitted so quickly from the spirits that you can receive a few sentences of information without consciously noticing how you received it. If you or your child are hearing voices and are being scared by them, then you will find the help you need to control this in the chapter on ghosts and spirits. Remember that you are always in control and you can demand anything of a frightening nature to stop immediately. You have an angel and a guide there for assistance and you will learn more about your spiritual team of helpers later on. For now, here is a fun exercise to try out with your child that can help you develop your telepathic connection to each other.

Telepathy – Send and Receive Exercise

To Send

You and your child can practise sending specific thoughts, words or phrases to each other and then check to see how accurate you both are. These thoughts can also be backed up with a visual image of the thought so that you are sending a picture. This will make the telepathy more powerful as you create the psychic vibration ready to send. In doing this you will also be using the gift of clairvoyance. An example of this would be if you were sending the thought form and word *orange* but then also back it up with an imagined picture of a piece of fruit, an orange. Visualize its shape and colour with as much detail, focus and concentration as you can. The more energy you put into your imagination and visualization, along with thinking the word orange will help you stand a good chance of your child picking up on this information.

To Receive

To be able to receive what is being sent to you, all you need to do is to create a space in your mind by bringing all of your awareness into the present moment. In other words, don't think about what you will be having for dinner later or what you did yesterday. To help you receive the telepathic information, you can create and imagine a large white cinema screen within your mind. Now inform yourself that you will be using this screen to receive the messages that are being sent to you. What you are actually doing is setting an intention to instruct your mind to prepare for your psychic practice. Intention is powerful and will help you to connect to your psychic senses. It is a fun game to practise and you can use your imagination to think of different things to create and send. Keep a journal and check to see how you both improve over time. For now, try sending pieces of fruit, shapes, colours and words.

The Psychic Ability of Clairvoyance

Clairvoyance is the gift to see clearly with the inner eye also known as the third eye chakra which is located in the centre of your forehead. It is through the activation of this chakra that clairvoyant images and symbols emerge to produce accurate psychic information. Such information can be actual or symbolic and it is a skill that needs attention, focus and practice to gain a level of accuracy. The good thing is though that you only need to start using it a few times to notice how accurate this ability is. Clairvoyance can be used to look into the past, present or future and is the forefront of psychic readings. By using clairvoyance you will be able to gain information quickly in the form of pictures or colours that can then be interpreted to find the answer you seek.

Clairvoyance can be used in healing, to scan the aura to see what the health of the physical body is like. This information can come through visual images of specific colours or shapes or anything that has form or energy that can be read and interpreted and thus healing can begin. In a later chapter I will include different ways to help you develop your clairvoyance naturally in a safe and controlled manner. You will also learn how to help heal yourself and your child. Clairvoyance can also be used by a medium to be able to see what a spirit looked like when they were alive and in their body.

They can then describe the spirit to their loved one having the reading so that they are able to recognise and validate them. This is amazing when very accurate information can be seen by the medium such as with a birth mark in a particular area, a tattoo of someone's name or a specific picture, a missing limb and even the colour of their hair etc. The list is pretty endless but the evidence that the medium can deliver is second to none.

Children who are clairvoyant will be very creative and interested in drawing, painting and art and craft work. They can also be deep dreamers and day dreamers and have an amazing imagination for story telling.

The Psychic Ability of Instant Knowing

This psychic gift is very subtle but very accurate and it can manifest in a couple of ways. Sometimes you will receive an *ahah moment* or what I call a light bulb going off above your head when you receive a brilliant idea. You may suddenly just know where the thing that you have been looking for is. Actually this happened to me today when I was writing this chapter. I was looking for a particular book I needed and I just couldn't remember where I had put it. After I looked through my entire wardrobe and in a number of places, I found myself thinking aloud "I wonder where I have put this book". Within an instant of asking this question I just knew where the book was. The information came so subtly to me that I had just experienced instantaneous knowing.

I found the book in my kitchen on the shelf amongst my cookery books and silently thanked whoever may have helped me. I believe your angels and guides can help you in this way and also your higher self, which is the very spiritual part of you. Maybe if I had just sat still and asked for help in the first place it would have saved me from getting frustrated in looking. Sometimes though, I am in too much of a hurry to remember the help that I have on hand. If you or your child has trouble finding something that you have misplaced, sit still and ask yourself 'where did I put my.....' then wait and see if you receive an instant knowing. If not, ask your guardian angel to help you find it and trust that they will do just that, and then have some patience. You will find out more about angels and the ways in which they can help you in a later chapter.

The Psychic Ability of Predictions or Reading the Future

This psychic gift is the ability to predict and foresee probable future events and opportunities. Predictions and reading the future is something that I am still quite good at today although I now know the future to be a set of probable or possible outcomes depending on the free will of the client's actions or lack of them. As a child I seemed to be able to predict things before they would actually happen. I remember telling my brother that our Dad was going to be working away from home. He had never done this before and sure enough a couple of weeks later our father had the opportunity of a six-week job away from home.

I remember as a teenager sitting under the school stairs with a few of my friends and reading their palms telling them what boys they would be dating and which ones would let them down. I wasn't actually reading their palms but by touching and focusing on their hands it helped me to create a psychic link and tune into their romantic futures. I also remember reading a complete stranger's palm when I was nineteen years old and working in a hair salon. Word had got out that I was psychic. As soon as I touched this woman and looked into her palm I instantly knew she was unhappy in love and would soon leave her relationship. I could also sense she would go to America and live abroad.

The woman confirmed everything I said and looked quite shocked that someone so young was so psychic. One older woman didn't quite believe that I was psychic and decided she would test me, she asked me when her daughter would have a baby. Instantly in my mind I heard the month of July and so I told her July. This was the due date of the woman's daughter and no one had been told that she was pregnant. I am glad to say that it wiped the smirk right off her face as she looked really shocked that I knew the answer. Psychics who want to strengthen their predictive abilities can use divination tools such as Tarot cards, Angel cards and Rune Stones. These tools can help to develop their intuitive mind so that they can begin to tap into the future and predict things. Future predictions can also be revealed to you during your dream state.

The Ability of Psychic Dreaming

The psychic gift of dreams can include premonitions, which are predictive in nature about events that are about to occur in your waking life. In this type of dream it can show you exactly what is about to happen as if you were actually there watching it unfold. When I was a teenager I dreamt that my boyfriend and I had broken up and he was now going out with one of my friends. When I awoke I could vividly remember this dream as it was quite emotional and it made me feel really sad. Within one week of my predictive dream we had a silly argument and we broke up and I just knew what was about to happen next. My dream then played out in my waking life exactly as I had already seen it and my ex boyfriend started dating my so-called friend. I feel that my predictive dream helped to prepare me for what was about to happen so that I could deal with my emotions. I still have predictive dreams occasionally although they have now become less frequent. I feel this is because I use my psychic ability daily and consciously and so I pick things up in my waking life instead of in my dream state.

Dreams that hold a lot of emotional energy are trying to tell you something, so it is best to pay attention to them. Write down in a journal what type of dream you have had and then go through each part of the dream and notice to see if anything springs to your mind about what the message may be. Once you have discovered the message that your dream is trying to tell you then you will stop any others from recurring. Another psychic gift in the dream state is when your spirit loved ones visit you. These dreams do actually include visitations from your loved ones who have already died. Spirit loved ones make their presence known and will communicate with you during sleep time. This is because it is easier for them to reach you when you are relaxed and in a deep sleep. In waking life you may be too busy or still grieving so much that you can miss the subtle signs that they leave you to let you know they are safe and well.

One main reason for the visitation is to let you know that they are ok and have survived death. Another is to help you through the grieving process so that you can begin to let go and move on. Sometimes your spirit loved ones will come with news of a pregnancy to come, or to gently let you know that they will soon be coming to meet Great Aunt Mary who is nearly at the end of her life. These spirit visits are special and amazing as you are actually connecting with your loved ones once again. Remember though that sometimes the dreams may make no sense to you at all but the essence is that your loved one came to see you and they are fine and well on the other side. You may see them exactly as you remembered them or they can appear younger and fitter with a beautiful glow around them.

Both my Nan and Grandad have visited me, which is brilliant because even though they died when I was quite young, I still miss them dearly and I feel it helps to keep us connected. I have also dreamt of other people I had known and who had recently died as they wanted me to pass on messages to their loved ones to let them know they were safe and still alive. As a medium the most important thing that my clients always want to know when they come for a reading, is if their loved ones are safe and happy. I also know that some spirits are so shocked with the fact that they have survived death that they want to let their family know they are still around them. They also feel more alive than they ever did when they were in their body. There are many times when I have been doing a reading and I bring through a spirit who initially didn't believe in life after death but now for obvious reasons does.

Sometimes it can be difficult for a spirit to reach their loved ones through their dreams for a number of reasons. This can be because of poor sleep patterns or for the fact that the loved one is grieving so much that they temporarily block out communication due to their emotions. This is only temporary but the spirit will try and get through someone else's dreams hoping that they will pass on the message from them that they are fine and well. Children are very susceptible to spirit visitations and they can often pass on messages to their relatives from the spirit who may have passed away even before they were born.

You can pray to ask for your loved ones to come visit you in your sleep and when the time is right you will wake up in the morning with fond memories of your amazing spirit visit. I do want to let you know one important thing and that is, even though you may not have any conscious memory of meeting up with your spirit loved one, this does not mean that it didn't happen; it's just that you can not remember it. We often visit the spirit realms during sleep to see our family and friends who have already died and this helps with the process of adjustment on earth without them. They have not gone for good, only their physical presence has disappeared but their spirits live on.

A Mixture of Psychic Gifts

Psychic children and adults will often use a mixture of psychic gifts but can be stronger in one or two particular abilities. I use all of them but I am stronger in the gifts of clairaudience and telepathy and this works best for me with my mediumship work. As a child I do vividly remember seeing a spirit child using *clairvoyance* and talking to her using *clairaudience & telepathy*. She was around the same age as me about five years old and I could also feel and sense her energy field using *clairsentience*. It felt like a slight force field and then she became see-through and transparent. She was a visiting spirit who came to say hello and play with me in my waking life. I felt that she may have belonged to my family in some way but she never said that herself. She didn't stay for long but it was long enough for me to remember her visit some 33 years later. Other psychic gifts that I have had are out of body experiences where my spirit went on its nightly travels to the other side. Have you ever been sleeping deeply and then you suddenly jump awake? This can be your spirit either leaving your body or coming back into your body but not as smoothly as other times and so you felt it.

My Psychic Childhood

As a psychic child I quite naturally accepted my abilities without question until I realised that not everybody had the same experiences. Now that I am older and I have studied the psychic and spiritual pathway in depth, the experiences that I had in my childhood now make a tremendous amount of sense. When I was little the psychic episodes I had just blended into the rest of my day and I never took time to distinguish between the world I was in and the messages that came from the spirit world. I was a sensitive child and could easily tune into other people quite naturally without any conscious effort too. I would use my feelings as a form of safety and preference of the people who came into my life and who I wanted to be around me.

I would stay away from anyone who made me *feel funny* inside. Sometimes I may have come across as being rude or shy but this didn't bother me at all because I trusted the way I felt within. Remember, that someone who is firmly in touch with their feelings will be using the gift of clairsentience. Clairsentients make great healers as they are able to feel and empathize with the pain of others. They find it easy to give compassion along with the healing energies needed. Healing is a big part of my life and I know the gift of clairsentience has helped me to help others who were temporarily stuck in their lives and with their health.

Good & Bad Vibes

I use my psychic vibes of clairsentience to see how I feel when I meet someone new for the first time. Good vibes make me feel safe and happy with a sense of being able to trust the person in my presence. If I get what I call bad vibes, I will then make my excuses and leave or if I cannot leave I will do what I can to protect myself, including my energy field. When I was little, if I was around anyone who was moody, depressed and angry or if someone had a problem with alcohol I would get negative vibes that made me want to protect myself. This was a total natural reaction for me to take even though at that tender age I didn't have any knowledge about auras and how we can absorb other people's negative vibes from their emotional or mental problems. I also now know that anyone who is out of balance with alcohol or drugs places themselves at risk of attracting an earthbound spirit who craves the sensations they can have through attaching to the person's aura.

This is so the earthbound spirit can experience the same highs as they used have on earth once more. More about this will be explained in a later chapter on Ghosts, including ways to protect you and your child. Maybe you had bad vibes about certain people when you were young and now that you are older you will understand why. If your little one shies away from certain people, then you need to trust the fact that they are using their natural clairsentient and intuitive abilities that are as real to them as the sky is blue. I have found that trusting and paying attention to my feelings is the best form of guidance that I have kept throughout my adult life. I have no doubt at all that in doing so has helped me to become the accurate psychic that I am today.

My first book called 'Feel the Vibes' explains how to trust your feelings vibes, to help you create success and healing in your life. Our feelings are the key to developing our natural intuitive nature. The way to develop your intuitive vibes is to become conscious of using them by checking in with how you feel every time you meet a new person or come across a new situation. In reading through each chapter of 'Psychic Children', it will help you to listen to and acknowledge your feelings *vibes* as well as understanding and honouring your child's feelings. Practise anything and you will always get better and become stronger and this is the same with your psychic ability. If you want to see results then you need to take the time to consciously practise and use your vibes.

Psychic Kids

Psychic Children will therefore display any or all of the above gifts and talents but they may not be aware of how to control them. They may also be fearful of talking to spirits or have even come across meddling spirits that are making them scared and they don't know how to deal with it. Other psychic gifts that can manifest with children are telekinesis, better explained as the moving of objects with the child's own psychic energy. Sometimes this is done without the conscious awareness of the child which can then be very upsetting for the parents as they fear it must be paranormal activity. Poltergeist spirits can cause havoc in the household but this is rare and there are ways to control this situation by calling in the help of an experienced medium who will know what to do.

Some Psychic Kids who remember their past lives will draw special memories of their past. One young boy kept drawing planes and he told his mum that he was a pilot in the war. Children who have had near death experiences have been known to draw special scenes on paper to show where they have been in Heaven. Children who are very creative may be clever at drawing spirit people or drawing the auras that they see around the people in their life. This is known as Psychic Art or Channelling. Other channelling gifts include automatic writing where the hand is controlled by spirit direction and words are written and formed from the spirit onto the paper. I remember I once did this and I received a message from my Nan saying 'remember me' To end this chapter I include spiritual terminology and descriptions and the different meanings of the array of psychic gifts so that you can familiarise yourself with them.

- Clairsentience – the psychic ability of sensing and feeling the vibes
- Clairaudience – the psychic ability of hearing with the inner ear inside your mind
- Telepathy – the subtle sense of receiving and transmitting thoughts.
- Clairvoyance – the psychic ability of seeing and receiving images and pictures with the inner eye known as the third eye
- Instant Knowing – the subtle ability of receiving instantaneous knowledge and information that just pops in your head.
- Psychic Dreaming – the ability to receive premonitions and accurate information of near future events
- Visitation Dreams – where spirit loved ones use your dream state to actually visit with you
- Predicting the Future – the psychic ability to foresee energy already set in motion to produce a probable outcome
- Aura – an energy field of current surrounding all living things; we all have an aura that contains our life force energy
- Psychometry – reading and interpreting psychic energy from objects, people and places
- Medium – a channel that can receive messages from the spirit world and then pass them onto those on the earth
- Psychic – the ability to read and interpret energy vibrations from people, places and objects. A psychic is someone who uses their sixth sense abilities

- Healer – a healer is simply a channel that is used for healing energies to be passed through and then to the person needing healing
- Higher Self – the spiritual part of us, our spirit, soul and essence
- Automatic Writing – the ability to channel messages from spirit through the written word. A form of trance is experienced by the person writing and often they will not know what they have written until they have finished
- Psychic Art – the ability to recreate and draw people who have died. Even though the word suggests a psychic ability, psychic art is a form of mediumship
- Telekinesis – moving objects with psychic energy
- Intuition – the ability to trust your feelings and vibes
- Ghosts – imprints of energy caught in time. Especially so, if the energy vibration left behind was from a traumatic passing. The picture of them remains but their spirit has crossed over into the spirit world. It can be likened to a video recording of an image caught in time.
- Earthbound Spirits – these spirits have decided to remain earthbound for their own reasons by avoiding crossing over to the light of the spirit world.
- Visiting Spirits – spirits that have crossed over to the light but can also visit with us and then go back to the light.
- Imaginary Friends – spirit children or guides that gather around children to keep them connected to the vibration of the other side. They are playful and helpful
- Angels – God's messengers that take our prayers, hopes and desires to God. We have our very own guardian angel and they will protect and guide us along our destiny.
- Guides – these are spirit teachers that can help us with our spiritual stud; they also help us to meet the right people who can assist us in our lives.
- Helpers – these are spirits that can assist you if you

require help for a number of different reasons. Our own spirit families will often want to help out in some way and will respond to thoughts sent out requesting assistance from above

- Meditation – when you take to time to connect with your spirit and source energy. You quieten the chatter of your mind and have time away from the problems of the material world as you relax in an altered state of awareness that brings you a feeling of inner peace. I would describe it as sleeping when you are awake.

Chapter Two

Psychic from Birth

'Don't you know that you yourselves are God's temple and
that God's Spirit lives in you?'
1 Corinthians 3:16

Born Psychic

In this chapter you will read stories about psychic children's
earliest memories and how our life on earth is planned prior to
us being born. Children have great imaginations, as did I, but
sometimes it is hard to know if some things they say are
imagined or are real. Once such thing I said to my family was
that I remembered being born. I know this sounds impossible to
believe and I have no proof whatsoever to back this claim up but
I do feel I remembered part of my birth. Even though the
memory has now gone, it is not forgotten. I recall being afraid of
the actual process of my being born in case it hurt me. I also
remember feeling the fear from my mother about my impending
birth but felt that it would hurt me more than it would hurt her.

I had an innate sense of knowing far more than a small baby
should know as my thoughts expressed this. Nethertheless,
when I was a lot older and told my family this over Sunday
lunch, they were in fits of giggles and disbelief and just thought
that I had a wonderful imagination. Sometimes it is all too easy
to dismiss what your child says as fantasy and make-believe,
but then you may actually miss out on something special. By
listening to and acknowledging what your child has told you,
you can help your child to have the confidence to tell you more
things when they happen. If you dismiss what your child says or
even tell them that they are naughty for making silly things up,

then you can confuse your child and they may also believe that they are bad. For obvious reasons this will do more harm than good in your relationship with each other and may also spoil the unfolding of your child's psychic senses.

We are psychic from birth because we are born with the spirit of God within us. We have unlimited potential to create our lives in whatever way makes our hearts sing by using our God-given gifts and talents. We are spirits having a human experience so that we may learn to become fully aware of our spiritual potential whilst in our bodies. When we wake up to the fact that we are spiritual in nature and our souls are eternal, then we become fully aware of who we really are whilst living life on earth. There are many people who are spiritually sleeping and live life only with the five senses. This life is not lived to one's fullest potential. Let this book be your wake- up call to incorporate the power of the sixth sense along with the importance of the five senses to live your life completely and successfully. In doing so you then have the secret power to heal yourself and your life and gain fulfilment of your dreams and desires. What a great example to set for a child to know that they have unlimited potential within them.

We forget we came from Heaven

The moment we are born a veil of forgetfulness exists for reasons of helping us to live fully in the here and now and allowing us to stay committed to our destinies. The spirit realm holds the most amazing and beautiful unconditional love and harmony – if we remembered how amazing life was back home, we may not want to commit to our spiritual growth when the going gets tough. Also if we remembered the challenges we had pre-planned to overcome on the earth then we would not gain full benefit of the experience from an unaware point of view. For this purpose, although there are many other reasons why we need to forget, we temporarily block out our pre-life memories. However some psychic children have the ability to remember certain insights about their prior existence and their connection with their spirit team of helpers.

Before a child is born to its chosen parents on earth, much planning and preparations are made ready for the spirit to integrate fully into their life. Such preparations include knowledge of the gifts they will need ready to live their life theme or destiny. They would have already decided what they intend to do and become and how they intend to help others in life. Service through the use of one's special gifts and talents to help others along their life paths will bring tremendous spiritual growth and rewards. When you help others unconditionally you will also receive any help you may need in your life. This is the spiritual law of giving and receiving and what you give out in energy, which is your time and service to others, will be returned to you.

Preparation for Life

Nothing is overlooked by the spirit to prepare and be ready for their new adventure on earth. Up until now they have been used to living in their most natural and loving environment in Heaven. They know that life on earth is sometimes difficult and they want to be on top of their game so to speak. If a spirit intends on becoming a doctor, for instance, then there will be a number of options available for them to prepare for their incarnation whist in Heaven. This will help them to succeed along their chosen path before they are even ready to be born. They may also look at alternative healing methods such as colour healing or crystal healing and their effects on the physical body. The spirit can choose to study specific medicines and the impact they will have to help heal others who are ill in their lives.

They may focus on specific types of human illness and find a variety of ways that they could help others to return to full health and well-being. Like I said, nothing is overlooked.

Advanced spirit helpers, including the spirits own chosen guide, will help to keep them on their healing path on earth. We all have a spiritual team of helpers to keep us right and help us to stay focussed on what we had pre-planned in the spirit world. It is all too easy to fall behind or to get caught up with the effects of life and then go off course a little. This is when our spirit team of helpers will interfere in our lives with gentle nudges and little wake- up calls so that we can adjust our future paths. We have already agreed to receive this help and guidance. What a relief to know, that all we need to do is send a silent prayer or request for help and our spirit team will hear us. Woo hoo!

Any kind of knowledge and wisdom that will help a spirit to achieve their desired goal will be available to them before they choose the time and date of their birth. Look to see what special attributes or characteristics are displayed by your little one. This may be a clue or sign as to what they are here to do with their life. My friend's boy has always had a fascination with airplanes since he was three years old. He loved to look at different pictures of planes and he had lots of airplane toys to play with. He told his mum that when he is a grown up, he is going to fly big planes across the sky. His mother once took him to an airfield exhibition and he was mesmerised by all of the old planes there and got really excited. He is sixteen now and is about to join the air force with the intention of becoming a pilot. His destiny was firmly grounded into his awareness and he must have meticulously planned his incarnation whilst in Heaven.

Birth Names

The spirit will now choose who their parents are, the place of their birth and also their own name. Astrology and numerology can provide incredible insights into a person's destiny. Every name and time of birth holds a specific vibration that helps to align the spirit with their life lessons and destiny. Some people will want to change their name when they are old enough because they find it too difficult to cope with the lessons that come with their specific vibration. This can be because they had not planned well enough beforehand or they have taken on more that they were able to handle. Some people will resort to using nicknames or will change their Christian name to their middle name or even assign themselves a name that takes their fancy. If you are interested in finding out more about yourself or your child's birth chart, then I suggest you find a professional astrologer who has gained much experience. They can be truly helpful with providing insights into a person's character, life purpose and their God -given gifts and talents.

By the way, if you think that you spent ages choosing the name of your baby, and so it must have come from you, then think again. Unconsciously you had not telepathically received the name for your child at that particular time. It is thought that the name of the future child is transferred from the universal consciousness into the mind of the parent. One of my clients was adamant that her baby was going to be called Amber. Once the baby was placed into her arms she said she knew instantly that she didn't look or feel like the name Amber. She felt like she was supposed to be called Lily, and in that instance she changed the babies name to Lily. This totally suited the beautiful baby girl. I asked her if Lily had been a previous choice for her, and she said no, it just came to her when she looked deep into her eyes.

Spirit Friends

Other plans made by the spirit prior to them being born include the friends they will meet up with and who will come into their life for a particular purpose. This can be for a number of reasons, as well as to help each other with a lesson or to keep each other company along life's path. We all need those special friends who love and support us if and when we need it. Have you ever had a feeling on meeting someone new that for some reason, you felt like you have known them all of your life. I have and I am sure you have too. This is soul recognition and you may very well be looking at one of your spirit friends from back home in Heaven. Special friends really do light up your life and they are the ones who love and support you and accept you for who you are. Special friends can last a lifetime or they can turn up at the time when you could do with one and they will be ready to assist you along your life path.

I have to tell you a story about my friend Cheryl. Cheryl I know is one of my spirit friends and the funny thing is, I can just imagine us having a conversation prior to our being born on how we would remember each other. I met Cheryl in 2007 when she attended a Psychic Development Course that I held from my home in Inverness. If you are meant to meet up with another person at a specific point of time on your life path, then the spirit world will help to work their magic so that both people's paths will cross. There are no such things as coincidences but there are plenty of synchronicities if you look carefully for them.

Cheryl

I placed a small advert in the local newspaper about the Psychic Development Course I was to teach at my home. Cheryl did not read this local paper but one of her friends did and she thought that Cheryl may be interested. Cheryl decided to ring me and after finding out about the course she booked to come on it. The very first day I met her I liked her immediately and felt we had a strong connection. I knew that she would become more than just a student but also a great friend. After the course we kept in touch and we soon realised how much we had in common. We were both born in 1971 and there are only two months between our birthdays. Both of our middle names are Sarah. Our great-grandmothers are both called Sarah and both of our brothers are called Jamie.

Yes, this sounds spooky, but there are no such things as coincidences, remember. I bet Cheryl and I thought about how many signs we could have so that we would recognise each other. Cheryl was also a Reiki Healer when we met and so was I, so we both had healing in common too. We both have freckles in the same pattern on the same arm and I am not joking about that one. We both feel that we have each other in our lives to support each other and be there for each other along our destinies. Do you have any friends in your life right now that you somehow feel soul recognition with? If so then you can be certain that you have both known each other much longer than the life you are now in. Spirit friends will come into your life for a number of reasons and you have both made all the prior arrangements before you even came to earth.

Spiritual Lessons

The spirit will also decide which lessons they would like to include so that they can have the emotional experiences from them that they would like to overcome. This can be anything from learning to be independent to overcoming some form of addiction such as smoking, alcohol or drugs. Again the list is pretty endless of what the spirit can experience and learn from. We must try to remember not to be the judge of anyone as we do not know the path they have chosen. Just because we would never wish to choose the same path does not give us the right to think we know what is best for them. If we do try and interfere in their life, then we may end up incurring some karma because we are preventing them from spiritually growing in the way they had wanted to.

It is only natural to want to help your loved ones when they are in emotional pain. Trying to actually stop the lesson when you know it could help them grow stronger and learn from it, will take away their achievement of overcoming it with their own spiritual power. You can always be there for them and offer your love and support, but know when you must let go and let them experience their life lessons themselves. Concentrate on dealing and overcoming your own lessons and then you can offer wisdom and life experience to others. Loved ones will then have the free- will choice to take your guidance on board or to do it another way. You may be exasperated as you can see the pitfalls they are about to go down, but it is their own choice to do so. Maybe after a few hiccups they will be willing to try things differently.

Only then the lesson can be learned from and will eventually dissolve. Help is always around and on hand, from Heaven above and from others along our life path. We have a lifetime to learn and experience many different things;when one thing is overcome we are then onto the next thing. Obstacles and problems are not as overwhelming when you realise that you always have spiritual help and guidance available to you. Remember this help is also within you, which is the power of your soul and by using your spiritual gifts of intuition and psychic vibes then you can begin to choose wisely.

Service to the World

Some spirits may desire to be some kind of leader in their life experience to offer great service by teaching or guiding others along their life paths. This is a hard path and one with many tests from the spirit world in order to make sure that you are responsible enough to reach lots of people. The negative about this choice is that you have to be careful that you do not allow your ego to get in the way of your spiritual goal. When success is achieved it can make you power- hungry and you can become absorbed with self-importance before the original intention of helping others. This will incur karma because the intention at the beginning was to help others but it shifted to self-importance and arrogance. So many people wish to become famous but being famous can bring very difficult lessons indeed which can set you back on your spiritual path.

Remember that service to the world comes in many different

ways from world leaders to toilet cleaners. What you need to know though is that all have equal importance to the Spirit World and no one is judged on what they wish offer the world. People are too easy to judge others in this world. Often those who have so called insignificant work are not acknowledged and are overlooked with providing a good service to others. We all affect each other and we all need each other to make our way in this world. A smile and a thank you can truly go a long way.

Mistakes & Hiccups

Mistakes are always made but there are always chances to rectify these and change them whilst in the body. Spirits do go off their chosen paths but they will always have the chance to get back on them. The Spirit World will try to gently influence the spirit to go back to their original plan but sometimes the spirit is too stubborn to listen. It will devastate the spirit when they arrive back home to Heaven to find that they didn't achieve what they had set out to. The spirit will want to make amends and will have to experience life again to learn what they had initially wanted to and also to be of service to those they may have negatively affected.

Now and again a spirit will be too eager to come to earth before they are really ready for such an experience and this can be overwhelming to their soul. They will experience many problems or obstacles that they had failed to prepare for due to the fact that they rushed to get here. Many of these spirits will have depression and be unfulfilled in their lives. They will also experience financial problems and have fears of not being safe and secure in the world. Basically they become off balance and feel lost and do not have the inner awareness to get back on track. All is not lost however because the Spirit World will try and reach the unhappy spirit through others. The Spirit World will bring others to assist them on their path and to help guide and teach them what they need so that they can make the most of the rest of their incarnation. It will be their own free will that will either keep them stuck or move them forward and this will dictate if they will be happy or live a life of struggle. We are responsible for our destinies and we must make an effort to change things if we are not truly happy. God will always help those who are willing to help themselves and we always have a spiritual team of helpers ready to assist us.

Spirit Team of Helpers

Our spirit team of helpers will be there for us whether or not we are actually aware of them and will work behind the scenes for us. Usually the spirit team of helpers consists of a guardian angel, a guide and spirit family and friends. The older you get, different guides can join your spirit team to help out with a particular situation, goal, obstacle or lesson. Generally speaking guides help to teach you something and angels are there to protect you along your life path, although both can do each other's tasks. Angels and guides can help to heal you when you are sick just as mine did when I had meningitis when I was only one year old. I do not remember this time though, except that during my early childhood I often felt dizzy with a funny feeling in my head.

Children can become more psychic after they have had an illness or an accident, especially if the head area is affected. When a child is ill or hurt they will also receive healing energies from their guardian angel, guides and spirit loved ones. This can help the child to form a stronger connection with their spirit helpers because of their illness or accident. I always knew that I was being encouraged in my life by someone who was not real to me, which meant *alive*. I can only describe this encouragement as being a helpful voice within my head that gave me good advice. This helpful guiding voice I later found out was my guardian angel. I felt that my angel was there to keep me company and to help me adapt into my new life and family. In receiving this help and guidance I would grow up with a good sense of the Spirit World and ready to fulfil my destiny. I totally accepted the voice of my angel without question and still do.

Although psychic children including myself do remember certain things about the spirit world, other memories will be vague to us. Again, this is to help us settle into life on earth and get on with our daily lives and existence. We have chosen to have an experience called life, and life is a gift that brings tremendous rewards. We need to be awake to life to take full advantage of this. In other words, wishing you were at home in the spirit world is not productive to living fully in the here and now and for this reason among many others, the veil of forgetfulness exists. However some psychic children, like Martin in the following story, can remember their time in Heaven even before they were ready to be born.

Martin can remember his life in the spirit world before he was born. He was three years old when he mentioned to his mother about his time in Heaven. The age of three is significant for many children to begin to discuss their psychic gifts. This is because the child now finds communication with their parents a much easier process for them to explain what they mean.

Martin's Story

Martin was three years old when he mentioned to his mother that he was good at drawing when he was in Heaven. He also said that he used to go to school there. At first his mum thought he had a great imagination and assumed he was making it up. Martin then went on to say that when he is older he is going to draw big buildings for people. His mum was amazed at this as this seems to fit in with the job of an architect. Martin's grandfather was an architect but he died when Martin was only a few weeks old. Martin is now eleven years old and he is still into his drawing and is very good at art in school. He doesn't remember what he told his mum when he was little. His mum is waiting to see if his chosen profession involves drawing big buildings for others.

Martin's story is unique in the way that his memories are of pre-birth. His matter-of- fact way in which he tells his mother about his prior existence shows his childlike innocence and the total acceptance he has of his life before life. The following story is about John who can remember hearing a helpful spirit voice.

John's Story

John was nine years old when he first encountered a spirit on coming home from primary school. He was walking home and was about to take a short cut when he heard a voice in his head saying, 'don't walk that way'; he ignored the voice and so once again he clearly heard the voice say 'don't walk that way'. This time he listened and turned around and went the longest route home. The next day at school he discovered that a strange man had been hanging around at the bottom of the lane and he had tried to abduct another child who had managed to get away. John feels that the voice belonged to his grandfather James who passed away the year before and is certain that he saved him from harm.

What an amazing story of love and protection from the grandfather, which goes to show that this still carries on even after death. I find these kinds of stories fascinating. In the following chapter you will read about psychic children's accounts with the angelic realm and the ways in which the angels can help you and your child.

Chapter Three

Children & Angels

'Angel of God, my guardian dear to whom God's love commits me here;
   Ever this day be at my side, to light and guard, to rule and guide.'
- *Old English Prayer*

Angels

We all have a guardian angel that has been assigned to us and given the special task from God to guard and guide us throughout our life on earth. Our angel is with us from the moment we first enter this world and will be there for us when it is our time to pass. We are never alone even when we think we are – our angel is always on hand. When we are low our angel will gently influence us with their loving healing energy. Their hope for us is that we may take notice so that we can begin to make wiser life choices. In this chapter you will read real life stories of angel encounters with children. You will also read about spirits who like to take on the role of being a protective guardian. You will discover ways in which to make contact with your very own guardian angel so that you can receive all the help and guidance you may need in your daily life.

What are Angels?

Angels are extremely high vibrational beings of light, a Divine Spark of God in the same way that we are a divine spark but they are a completely different species. Angels also have the role of acting as God's messengers between heaven and earth. It is said that the angels carry our prayers to God. As they are of such a high vibrational frequency of light, they are beyond our range of sight and sound and so become invisible and inaudible to us, except that is to psychic children. Psychic children's vibrations are faster and lighter than grown- ups' because of the purity of their spirit and consciousness and the fact that they have not long left the Spirit World. This purity keeps the vibes of the child extremely high and therefore the child becomes more adept to the sensitivity of the angelic realm.

Angels are neither male nor female as they are androgynous and beyond sexuality. However they can appear as a male or female influence so that you may feel more comfortable. Angels are recognised in nearly every major religion throughout the world. You do not have to be associated with any religion though to have a special relationship with the angels. There is a hierarchy of angels and all are assigned their own specific tasks. I include below the list of the different kinds of angels and the roles and tasks that they perform.

Guardian Angels – they are assigned to you before you are born to keep watch over you throughout your life on earth. Their role includes helping to keep you on the correct path that leads you to fulfil your destiny. They help you to reach your highest possible potential, gently encouraging you to believe in yourself when you lose confidence in your abilities. When you are sad they help to lift your spirits and give you healing. They also help you to meet specific people at the correct time along your life path that will be significant in helping you to fulfil your destiny. Finally they make sure that if it is not your time to pass then you will be saved from an early death or any harm.

It is wise to connect with your guardian angel to receive all the help, guidance and protection that they are able to offer you. 'Ask and it is given', - in other words you need to form a relationship with your angel as under spiritual law they are not allowed to interfere with your free -will choices. If you want this extra help in your life then you need to learn to ask for it. Many people miss out on this extra help as they are unaware of the power of the angels to assist them. People who have had near misses from an untimely death or accident may feel that they were helped from above or just somehow lucky, but you can be certain that their angel saved them.

Asking for Assistance

If you would like the help and assistance from your guardian angel or any of the Archangels listed below then all you need to do is send a silent prayer to the Angel of your choice. Ask them for what you would like help with and then trust that it is done. Your child could say 'dear angel of mine, please will you help me to stay focussed with my school work and help me to make some great friends, thank you'. Remember to be kind and polite by saying thank you as showing gratitude will help you to attract more amazing things in your life to be grateful for. Angels will appear with or be associated with a specific coloured light around them. Children can see this light and this can help them to recognise their angel. If you want to manifest a particular goal or desire then all you need to do is find the colour that is associated with the specific Archangel who is best to help you. Once you have the specific colour, you can then imagine and surround what it is you desire with this particular colour.

This is a form of visualization and it will also help you to feel and sense the vibration of the specific Archangel or angel. If you don't actually see or sense a colour for your own guardian angel then you can assign them your favourite colour and this will help you to connect with them every time you think of it. It is the intention that you have that will create your link to the angel. Only ever ask for any help and assistance if it is for the highest good and never try to ask the angels to help harm or hurt another. First of all the angels are angels of unconditional love and compassion and will never ever cause harm to another. Secondly you will create and incur some negative karma and this is the last thing that you would want to happen. Whenever I ask for any kind of help and assistance for myself, I always state that the help is to only be for my highest good. This is to ensure that if what I want is not really going to serve me well, then my angels will show me a better way.

The Archangels – these angels oversee the guardian angels and are of a higher vibrational frequency. Some Archangels help humanity with their special roles such as the following three who are the better known of the Archangels.

Archangel Michael – this mighty angel is the warrior angel who is able to protect you from negative energies and harm. You can ask this angel to help to give you some extra courage if you are fearful of something. Maybe your child is fearful of the dark, if so then you can teach him to ask this angel to help him to overcome his fears. When your child is going on a school trip or will be away from you for any reason then you ask for the extra protection of Archangel Michael to watch over them. Archangel Michael can also help you to cut any psychic cords that are no longer serving your highest good. These can be cords of addiction, depression, illness, eating problems or any negative traits and vibes that keep you living in your lower potential. Sometimes we carry over negative traits from past lives that we do not need or want to experience in our current life and so we can ask the mighty Archangel Michael to clear these old patterns within us.

When all of your family are going away on your holidays you can ask this angel to watch over and protect your family home and possessions. The colour that is associated with this beautiful angel is deep blue. I sometimes like to visualize myself surrounded by a deep blue imaginary cloak and this becomes my cloak of protection. Archangel Michael is pictured in art carrying a shield and with his sword of truth. Any of the visualizations that include the colour and these images, will help to connect you to the protecting energy of this particular angel.

Saying an angel's name three times will also help to connect you to the angel's vibration. Once you have done this, state your request and then thank the angel. Know that Heaven will do the best for you.

Archangel Raphael – this beautiful angel is the angel of healing, also known as the healer of healers. You can ask this angel to help your little one when they are sick. Raphael will help them to kick -start their own healing energies so they can return quickly back to full health and well-being. This Archangel will come through with a beautiful green light that will help to heal the physical body. You can also ask Archangel Raphael to surround your car with this green healing light when you and your child are travelling on a journey. Archangel Raphael can help you if you or your child, are having problems sleeping by helping to heal any emotional stress. This angel is also the angel of abundance and can help you to increase an abundant flow of finances towards you.

If you would like more prosperity in your life then this is the angel to assist you. Raphael will help you to find balance in your life through giving and receiving so that you create the vibration of prosperity. You can ask this Archangel for help with any matters of the heart or with your heart's desires. I imagine myself being soothed inside my body from my head to my toes with this lovely green healing light. You can imagine the green light entering the top of your head and pouring into every part of your body until it reaches your toes. You can also imagine the green light pouring outwards into your auric bodies, you will feel calm and balanced inside. Whenever I give a healing treatment to my clientele, I ask for the assistance of Archangel Raphael and visualize the angel's beautiful green light washing over my client. Often after having finished the treatment my clients remark that they could see a green light. This always makes me smile and confirms Raphael was with me and I silently thank this amazing healing angel for their help.

Archangel Gabriel –an amazing Archangel that can help you and your child to communicate clearly with each other. This Archangel will help to transmute negative energies and clear away any low or depressive thoughts. If your child has problems with reading or writing then Gabriel can help to bring clarity to their consciousness. If you would like help to become more disciplined with a particular goal or project then you can ask for this Archangel's help. Archangel Gabriel is associated with a beautiful white light and this colour brings purification to wherever it is needed. Imagine this white light enfolding and surrounding you and your child and ask that it help dissolve any stress or worries that may be affecting either of you. Archangel Gabriel can also help you and your child to develop your intuitive nature so that you strengthen your God -given gift to help serve you well in your life. I like to imagine myself surrounded in a bubble of sparkly white light that forms an egg shape around my body protecting my auric field. Make sure you see the light go underneath your feet and over the top of your head.

When you invite the angelic realm into your life, you will notice how your whole world begins to brighten up, leaving you feeling light- hearted and with a sense of joy and fun in your daily life. Angels can communicate to you through your intuition and help give you subtle nudges along your life path. Ask your angel for a sign that they are around you and then be open to receive this sign. One of the biggest signs is that they leave a white feather for you to find. This is their calling card and it can help you to know that an angel has just touched your soul. Later on you will read about other signs that they leave but for now make sure you keep a look out for a white feather. Remember that everyone has a guardian angel and it is never too late to begin a relationship with them; they have been with you from the minute you took your very first breath here.

A New Arrival

I remember as a child watching the Walt Disney film Dumbo about an elephant that had extremely big ears and could fly. In this film, a stork would deliver a newborn baby to its parents on earth. Any children watching this film would have the idea that the baby came from somewhere else first and was then delivered safely to the parents. This simple story is near to the truth of that film except for the fact that obviously the parents make the baby together but the soul arrives safely from the spirit world to join the newly formed baby. As it states in the bible we are created in the image and likeness of God, so our essence which is our spirit consists of the Divine spark of God.

This divine spark has tremendous creative potential ready for us to tap into and use in our lives on earth. Within this divine spark lie the powers of our sixth sense and psychic gifts. Once we are ready to begin our adventure on earth our angels act like the stork in the Disney movie and help us to arrive safely to our chosen mother so we can begin our new life.

Have you ever looked directly into a baby's eyes and thought to yourself how they seem to be so wise? Children are not born blank slates, as many people believe. They are born with full knowledge of who they are and the reasons why they are here and where they have come from. These reasons include their destiny and life purpose along with any lessons and challenges to be experienced and overcome whilst in the body. They also know that they have their own special guardian angel that will help to nudge them back in the right direction if they do go off track. Their angel has assured them that they will help to keep them safe from harm, accidents and illness if it is not a pre-chosen challenge by their soul. Soon the baby will start to lose most of the memories they initially have so that they can make the most of their life and destiny on earth.

An Angel's Touch

It is said that the small indentation between our nose and our lips was given to us by our angel when they pressed a finger there to help us forgot all the things we know from Heaven. We need to and agree to allow this temporary memory loss to happen for our highest good so that we can recreate heaven on earth by learning the truth of our true identity ourselves. It can be quite daunting for the baby about to be born as they are used to the loving vibrational energy of heaven and not the heavy atmosphere of the earth plane. Help and guidance is always available to the baby from their own personal guardian angel and spirit helpers. Their angel will be their support system to help them settle in with their new family, surroundings and environment. Encouragement and advice is telepathically filtered from the angel to the baby therefore making the baby feel at ease and able to adjust to life as quickly as possible. Preparation for the incoming life is given in the spirit world prior to the baby being born. This is to ensure they have a full understanding of the earth's vibration as it can still come as quite a shock to the newcomer.

When a Child Sleeps

When a baby or child goes to sleep they will continue to visit the spirit world so that they can remain closely connected to the vibration of home. They can visit with their friends and loved ones who have known them for eons of time. They will also meet up with their angel and guides and go over any issues they may have about their new life experience. Just because the baby may not be able to communicate properly on earth does by no means mean it has the same problems when they visit the spirit world. Their soul is not restricted by a small body or through the use of verbal communication and they have full awareness, function and spiritual wisdom on the other side. Many times spirit loved ones will also pay a visit to the earth plane to see the newly- born baby and to check on how they are getting along. Unknown spirits may also lend a helping hand by checking on the comfort and well-being of the baby. The following story has both kinds of visitations, one from a family member who had passed away before the baby was born and another from and old lady who was unknown.

Carole's Story

Carole and her partner Alan had just moved into their new home and Carole was pregnant with their first child. The previous owner of the house was an old lady called Maisie and she had recently passed away in the house. Carole and Alan quickly settled into their new home and soon after their new arrival came, a baby boy called Innes. When Innes was six weeks old Carole first sensed that there was a presence in their house. One particular day Carole heard Innes waking up and then crying through the baby monitor but then she also heard a male voice talk. Carole placed the monitor to her ear and as she did this she heard a man's voice speak again and Innes stopped crying.

Carole initially thought she must have been mistaken about the voice and so she didn't mention it to Alan who was out of the room at that time. Soon Innes started to cry again and once more she heard a man's voice talk to Innes and the baby stopped crying and started gurgling happily. Carole told Alan and they went straight upstairs to their baby who was lying awake and contented. Carole told Alan what she had heard over the baby monitor and explained that the voice was a very deep male voice. Alan commented that the only deep voice that he had known was his father's and his father had died in 2001 well before the baby was born. Both Carole and Alan found comfort in the fact that Alan's Dad was watching over their son.

They also found out that Innes had another spirit watching over him. Carole and Alan both heard the voice of a lady singing a lullaby to Innes and again this happened through the baby monitor. Carole believed this lady could be Maisie, the old lady who had previously lived in the house. Carole decided to do some research herself and also contacted me to see what spirits I could sense around her home. Carole discovered that Maisie's real name was in fact Mary and that she had never had any children of her own and had been a midwife for many years of her life.

When I tuned in to the situation I could sense an old lady and she told me her name was Mary and that it used to be her house. Mary told me that she never had any children herself and she confirmed to me that she liked to check in on the new baby in her old house. I also picked up that Alan's father often visited along with a grandfather called William. Carole confirmed that William was in fact her great-grandfather and was amazed at the evidence that backed up her own research. Both Carole and Alan are now firm believers that their child has spirit helpers who watch over him.

Carole seems to be quite in tune with her psychic senses as she has also received other signs from spirits. Once whilst sitting on her bed she heard her necklaces rattling on the bedpost from which they were hanging. She felt that it was Mary just letting her know that she was making a visit. As for the baby, Innes often stares at the corner lamp even though it is switched off and he smiles happily at it. Both Carole and Alan have smelt perfume in the air and their lights have switched on and off by themselves. All these signs are from the child's spirit guardians who are happy to make their presence known. This story goes to show that the new baby has a team of helpers acting in the role of a guardian, just like their own angel. These helpers will come and go but their guardian angel is always on hand.

Carole's experiences with the baby monitor are not that exclusive, I have received many letters about spirit voices being picked up via the baby monitor. One story that I received is short and sweet as it involves a beautiful conversation between a little boy of two and his angel.

Myles

Myles is a sweet- natured child who is always happy and as his mother would say, quite a little chatterbox. Myles has never had a problem going to sleep at night and would happily take his cuddly toy rabbit with him when his mum said it was his bedtime. His mum would gently tuck him in and kiss him and his rabbit goodnight and then turn on the baby monitor. She would then go to the kitchen to make her nightly cup of tea and sit at the table to drink it, the baby monitor near by. Often she would hear Myles talk to himself but one evening she heard Myles have a full conversation with what she can only imagine was his guardian angel.

The conversation began with Myles saying yes then a pause then another yes followed by another. His mum instantly felt that he was answering someone's questions so she turned up the volume of the monitor to listen. Myles was telling whoever he was talking to that he had been playing in the garden with his ball. He then started laughing and said he was going to see the animals tomorrow. As his mum listened she then heard him say 'ok goodnight angel, love you' and then he went to sleep. In the morning his mum asked him who he was talking to the night before and he answered my angel friend, she looks after me.

What a beautiful story. It is normal for a little one to have such clarity of communication with the spirit world. This is especially so when the child is a natural at communicating, just like Myles is being a little chatterbox himself. Myles is now six years old and he doesn't remember the chats he had with his angel but his mother reminds him and this makes him smile. Myles still talks to his angel whenever he needs help or if he is afraid of something as he believes his angel will help him. This has definitely kept his psychic link with his guardian angel open for angelic intervention.

Angelic Intervention

There is nothing that is too much trouble or too intricate for the angels to help with and intervene. This includes intervening in events prior to them happening to prevent great danger or untimely death. Angels can intervene in whatever way they choose so that they can affect a subtle change that can then alter the outcome of a situation. They did this for my husband and me when we were on a drive to visit a friend in Aberdeen. The angels are all- knowing and as their job is to guide and protect they are fully aware of all events ahead of us even if they are minutes, days, weeks or months away. This is my story of angelic intervention. So many times the angels will step in and save you from harm without you even being aware of it.

Jock and I were looking forward to visiting our friend for lunch in Aberdeenshire as we both used to live in the area but now we lived a good two hour drive away. During our drive, we decided to stop for a coffee break at the garden centre along our route. After our coffee we got back into our jeep to carry on with our journey and found that our jeep just wouldn't start. We sat there wondering what on earth was wrong as this had never happened before and our jeep was practically new and in excellent condition. We tried again and this time it started and I actually said to my husband that maybe that was meant to happen to delay us from having a crash. I know that every thing happens for a reason and I felt that this happened for a reason. We began our journey again and after driving for a few minutes along the country road we noticed a car overtaking a long line of cars.

The car was now in our lane and heading towards us at full speed and was running out of space to get back in. There was literally no space to our side to pull over and other cars started beeping their horns at this crazy driver. I began panicking as it looked like we were going to have a head -on crash. With seconds to spare the car swerved to the front of the traffic and amazingly had just missed us. I know beyond a shadow of a doubt that if our jeep had started immediately as per usual then we would have been a minute ahead or so along the road in a head- on car crash. It could have easily been fatal. I thanked the angels out loud and I was also grateful that I was able to notice the angelic intervention that quietly played out in both of our lives without any mysterious happenings. Later that day we found a white feather and this also helped to confirm our angelic assistance. I feel blessed to have received Heaven's help that day. Have you had any close calls that seemed to just pass you by? Then if so you have surely been touched by an angel. The next story is about angelic assistance for a little girl who was afraid of the dark.

Kellie-Ann's Angel

This story was sent to me by a lady called Florence who says she would love to share her own experience of a visitation to her daughter from her guardian angel:

"Kellie-Ann would have been between the age of three and four, one night whilst sitting up in bed giving my little son Andrew his two-o'-clock feed, I suddenly focussed on light voices coming from my daughter's bedroom. Almost whispers......then the most joyous giggling.......you know that real chuckle when a child is wondrously happy and it makes you smile too. My daughter was not for sleeping in her own bed when the thought of our big cosy brass bed was calling her in the dark of night. I saw her reflection in her bedroom mirror as she crossed the hall into our room. She had such a smile on her face and she was heartily waving goodbye to someone. Not knowing if she was awake or sleep walking and still dreaming,

I was unsure what to say or do.

She carefully climbed into our bed over her dad and said to me 'my mummy is gone' I said 'I am your mumm' 'yes I know' said she 'but my other mummy, the one with the white long dress'. At that, she turned over and went to sleep. I was left with goose bumps and the hair on the back of my neck stood on end. Is it possible that because she was so afraid of the dark that her guardian angel stayed with her until her usual stroll into our room at two-o'-clock! Was this the last time she was going to see her angel? I didn't know but what I do know is that she needs her angel so much at the moment. Her wonderful brother whom she was so close too and loved dearly is now in the spirit world. She needs all the help her guardian angel can bring her and I have humbly asked her angel to help my daughter through this painful grieving time."

This story brings up two important issues of protection and healing. Guardian angels and spirit helpers will offer both of these services to help us in our time of need. For children who are afraid of the dark, angel guardians will draw close to them to help keep them safe from their fears and insecurities until they fall asleep. It is wise to teach your child that they have a guardian angel and include the ways in which their angel can help them in their daily lives. Your child will become more confident and independent knowing they have their own very special angel who is like an invisible best friend. They can tell their angel about any inner fears and worries they may have. By releasing these fears and worries to their guardian angel then they are releasing these low emotional and mental vibes that affect their self-esteem and confidence. They will soon become stronger in character and less fearful. There are many different ways that the angels can let you know that they are with you. Check out the following signs and then you can teach these to your child.

Signs from the Angels

Remember to ask for one.

White feathers – these can float down in front of you from out of nowhere and even manifest themselves around your home.

Films – maybe you have decided to watch a film and are unaware that it includes an angel in the film or other references about angels in the film. Maybe there is a special message in the film for you or it will be to confirm that your angel is with you. A classic film that includes an angel who is called Clarence and is one of my favourites is 'It's a Wonderful Life'.

Music – maybe you have asked for a sign and then turned on your radio and the very next song you hear is a song about angels. A well known song is Angels by Robbie Williams.

Clouds – on asking for a sign you may glance up to the sky and there for a couple of seconds is the most amazing shape of angel's wings. This is a great sign but you can doubt what you have seen as it doesn't last very long. The thing to remember is that you asked for a sign and got one.

Angel Pins – on asking for a sign you may find that a friend or relative has bought you a lovely angel pin to place on your coat. The thing is though that they didn't know you asked for a sign but your angel did.

Butterflies and Birds – notice to see if any butterflies or birds are especially near you as these are also signs from the angels. Angels will send you these lovely winged creatures to let you know they are near.

A gentle breeze – maybe you have asked for your sign and then you feel a gentle breeze pass you buy that just ruffles your hair or brushes along your face, making it tickle. Your angel is surrounding you with their wings.

Numbers – if you come across the numbers 444 not long after you have asked for a sign then this is a sign that thousands of angels surround you. Whenever it is 4.44pm on my mobile, I quickly say hi to the angels as I know they are near.

Warmth – you have asked for your sign and then you suddenly feel a lovely warm feeling encompass and surround you. This is another angel hug.

An Actual Appearance – you have asked for a sign and you may be one of the lucky ones who could actually get to see an angel. This is quite rare as the angels will use all of the above signs and many others first as they are easier to manifest because they belong to our world. However the angels may show themselves if they feel they need to and this does not have to be with wings and the normal association you have of what an angel should look like. The angel may also come to you in your dreams or in the form of a complete stranger. This quote from the bible lets us know that there are angels amongst us.

Don't forget to be kind to strangers. For some who have done this have entertained angels without realizing it.
- Bible - Hebrews 13:2

There can be many more signs than this and it is up to you to notice them once you have asked for a sign off your angel. The signs are there to help guide you and keep you aware of what you can expect to find but are by no means exclusive. Angels also help us to remember who we are and what we are capable of achieving in our lives. To know that you have your own personal angel to help you throughout your life can be liberating and heart -warming. In fact, no matter how lonely you may feel in your life you are never truly alone and all you need to do is to invite and ask your angel to help you. Start today and ask your angel to enter your life, ask them for a sign that they have heard you and soon you will receive the evidence that your angel is around you. Either you can ask aloud or inside your mind, it makes no difference. To finish this chapter I will leave you with an exercise for both you and your child to help connect with and contact your guardian angels.

Practical Exercise – Meet with your Guardian Angel

First of all find a nice quiet place where you and your child will have peace to do this exercise. It won't take you long to do and it is a fun exercise that may also help you to receive the name of your guardian angel. You can read through the exercise first and then remember what you need to do so you can both do the exercise together. Or you can read it out to your child after you have had a go yourself.

Imagine a beautiful white light surrounding you and ask your child to imagine this light around them. You can visualize this light around you by intent if you are having troubling using your imagination. Intention is stating something and knowing with faith that it is done. Visualize this light coming to you from high up in the sky and slowly falling around you from your head to your toes. See this light form a bubble around you in the shape of an egg from under your feet to over your head. This light is the light of the Holy Spirit and will protect you from negative vibes and low- level spirits. You can even ask aloud that you would like to receive the protection of the white light of the Holy Spirit to surround and protect both you and your child. I do this daily anyway whether or not I am doing any visualization exercises.

Now imagine that you are about to leave though your own front door. As soon as you walk through your front door you find that you are in the most beautiful garden that you have ever seen. You then notice a lovely white bench shaded under a great big tree and surrounded by the most amazing flowers which are vivid in many different colours. Go and sit on this bench and take in the pleasant surroundings. You feel safe, happy and at peace where you are. Your guardian angel is about to join you by sitting next to you on your bench begin to feel your excitement build inside you. Soon you feel a gentle breeze brushing past you and it is a sign that your angel has arrived. Look to the side of you immediately and make a mental note of what your angel looks like. Do they have a certain colour, feeling or shape? Do they have wings or are they dressed as a male or a female? Take notice so that you remember later.

Ask your angel if they will give you their name and make a mental note of what you receive. Do not worry if you feel you are making it up, just take note of what you are seeing, feeling and hearing. Finally this is your opportunity to tell your angel anything you would like to or maybe there is something you would like their help with. Notice what their response is, maybe it is an overwhelming feeling of love and support but no communication. Now it is time to thank your angel and leave the garden to make your way back to your home. You do this with intent and by opening the front door to your home and closing it behind you. Once you are ready, write down on paper the colour of your angel, what they looked like, their name or any thing else your angel may have said to you.

Do not worry if you didn't get a name this time as you can just call them angel. Also you may receive their name on another go doing the same exercise. You can use this exercise anytime you want to speak to your angel; this can be your own special place. Remember you are the creative artist of your own imagination and you can make your special place as unique to you as you would like. In other words, maybe you would like to see some animals there or a waterfall or any other thing that makes your soul sing. If your angel appeared with a particular colour, then you can imagine this colour forming near you whenever you need to connect with your angel in your daily life. Imagine their colour surround you and then communicate to your angel via this psychic link. In the next chapter you will read about ways to strengthen your child's intuition. This can help them to be sensitive enough to pick up any messages from their angels and their higher self. Developing intuition can also help to strengthen the psychic bond between the mother and child.

To end this chapter I will leave you will a little angel prayer that I was taught in junior school and I have said this prayer daily ever since.

'Lord, keep us safe this night, secure from all our fears: May angels guard us while we sleep, Till morning light appears.'

- *John Leland*

Chapter Four

Intuitive Children

'Follow your instincts. That's where true wisdom manifests itself.'
Oprah Winfrey

The Intuitive Child

Intuition is an important psychic gift that if developed and understood can truly help both you and your child within your daily lives. Encouraging your child to check in with their intuitive feelings as they grow into adulthood will be one of the most valuable tools you can teach them. In this chapter you will learn ways in which to trust *your own vibes* so that you will know how to teach your child to trust and strengthen theirs. You will also read true stories about children who are highly intuitive and sensitive. There will also be a practical exercise included to help build up your confidence when using your vibes. You can teach this intuitive exercise to your child.

All children are intuitive and some can be extra- sensitive to the many different energy vibrations around them. The environment in which they live along with their family members, home life, friends and pets will all in turn have some kind of effect on the child. This will be explained in greater detail in a later chapter on healing. Another way in which a child's intuition will manifest itself is through clear insight which can be about a person, situation or problem. In other words the child will experience a greater perception about the unspoken needs and feelings of family members, pets and also pick up on whatever resistance is showing up as a problem. They are able to tune into the energy of the problem and have the insight to know what the best solution may be. The child can receive subtle messages that will enter their mind that contains instantaneous knowledge for them to understand. They can then voice their concern or offer help and guidance because of the feedback they have been receiving from their intuitive vibes.

Adults can overlook and ignore the clear insight of the child and may miss out on any help or information that would help and assist them. For instance a child may announce that granny is unwell or their pet is hurt, even though it may not be easily noticeable to the grown-up. They may also offer insight into a particular problem because they can feel the resistance to it, such as when mum is stressed out because she cannot find something important. The child will subtly feel the irritating emotions expressed by their mother and will then be able to tune into whatever it is she has misplaced. Maybe the mother has misplaced her car keys and the child will then let her know where the keys can be found. This is great if the mother pays attention to her little one, otherwise she may become more annoyed still looking and wasting her time.

A client of mine misplaced her passport as she was certain it was in the kitchen drawer at home but when she looked it was no where to be found. She soon started to get stressed out thinking of where it could be and if she had thrown it out by mistake. Her little girl walked into the kitchen and said outright 'your book is in your bedroom' At first my friend didn't connect the book with the passport so she didn't take notice of her daughter. Then she realised her daughter was trying to help her so she asked her what book did she mean and her little girl said 'the book you are looking for' My client found her passport at the top of her wardrobe in the bedroom.

She gave her daughter a big hug and asked her how she knew where her passport was. Her daughter said 'I felt it was there when I was playing with my toys and you were worried because you thought you lost it. Then I saw a picture of your bedroom in my mind and just knew it must be in there'. The feelings her daughter had are connected to the intuitive bond that she shares with her mother. Insight about the matter was received via clairvoyance, just like the little girl said, with a picture popping into her mind.

Intuition

Intuition is also known as the sixth sense and everyone has this psychic ability but just like learning to ride a bike, it is better to start acknowledging it when young. If any of you have read my first book on psychic development, called *Feel the Vibes*, you will know that is was around the age of eight that I consciously became aware of my intuition. Intuition is a knowing and feeling sense which is part of our sixth sense, and if listened to and developed can help to steer us along in our lives. Paying attention to our intuition can also help to keep us safe from harm by preventing us from making unwise decisions and choices or alerting us to danger. When we learn to trust our intuitive nature we end up making wiser life choices which bring about a brighter future. Our angels and guides often use the gift of our intuitive nature to communicate with us through gentle influ-ences to help us change direction and with inspirational ideas. It is our free will to pay attention to this divine help or to ignore it.

The best and most wonderful advice that I can offer you right now would be to start helping your child develop and enhance their intuitive nature. A child who is in tune with their intuitive side will hold the key to help them create a life that is fulfilled, safe and happy. They will know they have unlimited potential and will find harmony in their lives by trusting their intuitive nature. They will also know that when they feel bad vibes they can alter their path, preventing possible danger so they can protect themselves. It is never too late for you to discover the benefits of using your intuition to enhance your sixth sense. In doing so you will have discovered a new way to live that can help you in all areas of your life.

Intuition has many different ways in which it expresses itself and one of these ways is to *just know something*before the evidence has been revealed to you. You may have come across this yourself in times such as knowing who was calling on the phone before you answer it or knowing you would bump into an old friend that day. The following short story reveals how Emma *knew* her Grandmother was coming for a visit even though no one expected to see her as she was supposed to be on holiday in Italy. Here is Emma's story written by her mum Mandy.

Emma's Story

"Emma was four years old when she started to tell me things that she could not possibly have known. One time she told me that Grandma, my mother, was coming over for a visit even though her Grandma was in fact on holiday in Italy and not expected home for another few days. To be honest I didn't take much notice as I thought she was confused about the fact my mum was still away and maybe she was just missing her. A mere half- hour later the doorbell rang and I opened the door to see my mum standing there. I was a little spooked to see her as Emma had known she was coming. Mum told me that she had become ill on holiday and had gotten an early flight home. She said she didn't want to cause any fuss or worry by letting us know, and her flight home was straightforward. I asked Emma how she knew that Grandma was coming, and Emma said 'I just knew it and I felt her'. Emma is seven years old now and we still talk about this story at family gatherings;in fact it has opened up our minds to know that something bigger exists. Emma and her Grandmother are particularly close and share a special bond and I wonder if this is why Emma knew that she was about to visit."

A Mother's Intuition

Special bonds exist between parent and child and a mother's intuition can alert her to her child's needs. Mothers and daughters can develop an amazing bond that in adulthood can blossom into a deep friendship. They display signs of knowing what the other one is feeling and will say what the other one is thinking. Soul- mate relationships are also like this, along with twins and siblings who are extremely close. Soul- mate relationships do not have to be of a romantic connection; they can exist between father and son, grandmother and granddaughter or best friends and so on. These special bonds will create a psychic connection enabling each person to tap into and know what their loved one is thinking, feeling or experiencing.

I have a strong telepathic connection to my mother and my husband Jock and every so often we are amazed at how we are thinking of exactly the same thing at the same time. My mother is definitely intuitive and we have a close connection and soul - mate relationship. I feel that we have been together before in a past life; you can read more about past lives in the following chapter. My mother is the one who has helped to teach me to rely on myself and follow my heart and I am extremely grateful for all of her love and support. My mother has had intuitive dreams about me and has also heard a spirit call her name and wake her up from her sleep. We can feel each other's moods and emotions and we are very much alike in character. My mother is amazing when faced with a crisis and just gets things dealt with and sorted and this strength shines through her spirit. Mum has always been there for me when I have been ill or have had an accident and we share a strong psychic connection. Look for the intuitive connection you share with your own mother or children- you can make this stronger by sharing each other's thoughts and feelings. The intuitive connection you share will also carry on beyond physical death. The following story shows the intuitive connection shared between a mother and her son.

Stephen's Story

Stephen is four years old and has a close connection to his mother. His mother bought him a pet parrot that they kept in a large cage in the back room of their house. One afternoon when Stephen was taking a nap, his mother noticed that the parrot had escaped and was sitting in the tree in their back garden. His mum was trying to gently catch the parrot to place him back in its cage and was having some trouble in doing so. Eventually she managed to get hold of the parrot and soon it was placed safely back in its cage. As soon as Stephen awoke he said to his mum 'I helped you catch the parrot' His mum was surprised at this as there was no way that Stephen could have seen what happened from his bedroom, and he was in a deep sleep. His mum asked him how he knew that the parrot had escaped and what did he do to help her catch it. Stephen said that he feltshe needed help to catch the parrot and so he came to help her when I was at the tree. There was no way that Stephen could have known this and it is amazing to think that her son was able to help her when he was sleeping. She feels the close connection betweenthem daily but this was the first time she was aware of how deep that bond goes during sleep time.

Intuitive Feelings

What a lovely story that shows the intuitive bond between the parent and child. Intuitive bonds are shared when emotions and feelings expressed by the mother are then received by the child or vice versa. Understanding and acknowledging the ways in which the intuition expresses itself is an important aspect of learning to trust your vibes. Intuitive feelings can be produced internally with our emotions or with physical sensations of the body. Maybe you have heard someone say that they had a gut instinct of some kind, and as the word gut suggests the feeling is expressed in the stomach area. The stomach is an area where you can feel excited or nervous and when someone is in the early stages of love they may get what is known as butterflies in the tummy. These physical sensations can come in flutters and waves of excitement as they feel the person's energy they are in love with having an effect on them. Check the list below for some of the ways that you and your child may be unconsciously using your intuition. The more you become aware of your intuitive nature the stronger it will become.

Feel the Vibes

We all have an aura which is our energy field and is made up of our physical body and spirit. In fact all living and non living things have an aura and because of this whenever our energy field encounters another's energy field then an energy exchange can take place. In experiencing this energy exchange you will receive information through your intuition and it can be felt emotionally or physically. These are some of the ways in which you can feel the vibes.

*Funny feelings in the tummy area

*A warm or cold reaction all over

*The hair on our body standing on end

*Our muscles twitching

*Goose bumps

*Breaking out in hives or some skin condition

*Headaches that arrive when you are with someone negative and go as soon as you go away from them. This can also happen if you visit somewhere where there is a lot of negative energy and especially so if you or your child are extra sensitive.

*We can shiver or have a change in breathing and even palpitations

*We can feel an overall feeling of uneasiness

*You will just intuitively know the answer to something

*You can receive insight out of nowhere about a problem

*You can receive inspirational ideas to start something new

Your higher-self, angels, guides and spirit loved ones will all try and gently influence you in these ways by using your intuition. Acknowledging our vibes will help us to understand the subtle signs around us. We are constantly receiving feedback through our energy field and how amazing is that when we begin to learn what our vibes are telling us. We become powerful creators in our lives when we pay attention to how we feel we start to make wise choices as we learn how to trust our selves. We also open up our vibes to receive heaven's help with their inspirational ideas to create great things in our lives.

Every time you listen to your intuition, you build your psychic muscles and create confidence in your ability to feel the vibes. You also become more sensitive, enabling you to become your own inner radar system that provides you with clear insight for your highest good. For those of you who did not read my first book, I will quickly explain what happened to me around the age of eight that ignited the awareness of my intuitive spark.

My Own Intuition
I had been having a drink of orange squash and had some left over so I placed my plastic cup half- full in the fridge. A few hours later I decided to go back and drink it and on opening the fridge door I instantly knew not to drink my squash as there was a spider floating around in my drink. How did I know this? I had not even looked inside my cup. I felt an overall sense of knowing not to drink it without looking inside first because there was a spider in there. Then I looked in and I saw a spider floating about in my squash. I swear I didn't know what I was more shocked about, the fact that a spider was in my drink as I am not too keen on spiders, or the fact that I knew about it before I even looked. I screamed and dropped the squash and that was the first time I became consciously aware of the sixth sense and my intuition.

Children's Feelings

A psychic child is very open emotionally and is quick to tell you how they feel. They can sometimes have a tantrum or come across as stubborn as they do not like doing anything that makes them feel off- balance and will soon let you know about this. They will act fine around certain friends and family and will not be themselves around others. This is because they find it easy to tap into the aura and energy of a person which lets them know what the real person is like and not what they pretend to be. It doesn't matter how much someone pretends to be happy or nice, their true self will always be felt in their energy field and this is what a child will feel. Notice to see if your child feels uneasy vibes around certain people. They may be trying to tell you that they do not want to spend their time with them and can act all shy or stubborn to display this to you. Please note that just because your child has uneasy vibes does not mean that the person is bad in anyway. It is most likely that the child will be feeling the energy of the person that maybe needs some healing or help and is hiding it.

Do not force your child to cuddle or kiss anyone they do not wish to just because you want them to be sociable. They will show you themselves who they are happy enough to be comfortable with. If you do make them go against their own inner feelings then you are participating in helping them lose touch with their intuition. Remember their intuitive nature is an invaluable psychic gift for keeping them safe in their future. If your child does not feel comfortable with anyone then these feelings need to be honoured even if you feel totally comfortable with the same person. To encourage your child's natural intuitive nature check in with how your child feels about specific things and notice to see if they are correct. Remind your child to use their feelings whenever they do anything new. Your child's ability will soon flourish. The following exercise is helpful for both you and your child to strengthen your intuition. It is a very simple exercise that is purposely written to help you recognise the feelings you get from outside circumstances. Most of the time feelings go unregistered and are ignored and mistakes can be made through lack of better judgement so to speak. When you bring your feelings into your conscious awareness and acknowledge them, then you will have your full power available to make an instant decision that is for your highest good.

Practical Exercise to Enhance your Childs Intuitive Nature

You will need a journal to record your thoughts and feelings and to keep track of your progress. This is a great exercise to do together, encouraging your child to write down their feelings also but if they are too young then you can do this for them.

*First you need to imagine something that makes you feel very happy inside- it could be a special memory of some kind or it could be a special event or holiday. Now really get into this happy feeling with all of your being. Pretend that you are actually back in that happy place and feel the joy build inside you. Notice and write down anything that accompanies this happy feeling, such as a warm feeling inside or a feeling of excitement in your tummy like the term *butterflies in the tummy.* Pay attention and write down every happy feeling you get.

*Next you need imagine something that makes you feel fearful inside. Maybe you are afraid of spiders or afraid of the dark. Maybe you are afraid of heights etc. Again *feel* how this affects you with your emotions and notice to see if you have any physical responses to your body. Does the hair on the back of your arms and neck stand on end? Do you feel cold all over or even get a shiver run down your spine? Are your fists clenched tightly when you think of something you don't like? Again you need to write down every fearful feeling you get.

*Compare your two different lists of feelings and any bodily sensations that you got. Your intuition is now building up a psychic alphabet inside you. It will store your registered feelings and reactions to be able to give you subtle signs and clues when meeting new people or coming across new situations for the first time. When I am fearful, I get cold and shivery and feel nervous tension inside. I take note of what I am feeling and make any immediate changes that I need to. I also pray to my guides and angels for their protection and guidance.

*Now, based on those feelings, whenever you do something new or meet someone new listen to what your vibes are telling you through your feelings. This is the heart over the head matter. The more you rely on your feelings the more intuitive you become. Remember: feelings equal intuition. Get used to asking your child how they are feeling inside. Nerves and excitement aside, you will soon discover that your feelings are an indicator of the truth. Children are able to intuitively tell a good seed from a bad apple and so if they keep in check with their feelings then they will carry this important skill with them throughout their life. To learn more about trusting your intuition to work for you, check out my first book called 'Feel the Vibes'. I cover this subject in greater depth.

The following chapter will take a look at children's past lives.

Chapter Five

Children's Past Lives

'I did not begin when I was born, nor when I was conceived. I have been growing, developing, through incalculable myriads of millenniums. All my previous selves have their voices, echoes, promptings in me. Oh, incalculable times again shall I be born.'
Jack London, The Star Rover

Past Lives & Reincarnation

Many young children throughout the world spontaneously recall memories of their past lives and their reincarnation without any kind of regression or prompting from an adult or therapist. Much of what they remember and the ways in which they can describe specific details at such a young age are astounding. These children would not have had any way of knowing about such details that happened prior to their current existence. The children who have these past life memories have them quite naturally and will spontaneously come out with things such as *my other mummy used to sing to me every night but you tell me stories.* It is absolutely amazing what can come out of the mouths of these babes and youngsters.

Children's past life memories are now being researched and accepted all over world and there are plenty of informative websites and books on this subject if you are fascinated by it. The special message that these children help to teach us is that there is life after death and we exist beyond the confines of our physical body. Life is eternal and our soul lives on when our body dies and disintegrates. Love is what is left over and this love carries on into the spirit realm and then into our new future lives. Children who believe they have lived before will often reveal intricate past- life memories that include instances such as remembering who they once were, where they previously lived and ,startlingly, how they eventually died.

Children's memoires of their past lives can range from very detailed and vivid accounts to short and sweet momentary recall. One little girl simply mentioned to her Dad one day when he picked her up in his arms, *if he could remember when he was a little boy and how she used to pick him up in the same way. One little boy said to his mother that he was much happier in this life with her as they didn't have to hide under the bed anymore.* This kind of memory is short and sweet and once mentioned by the child it is usually forgotten pretty quickly. If you have a child who has also said similar things then try not to miss out on the moment and gently ask them if they can remember anything else about their past life. I would also suggest that you record these memories down in a journal because as the child ages their memories usually begin to fade and then eventually stop. Below is a compiled list of some significant memories of children's past lives.

A Variety of Past Life Memories

*Remembering their first name from a previous life time and sometimes even their full name.

*Remembering their parents' and siblings' names from their previous past life.

*Remembering where they used to live. This can sometimes be the street they lived on or the house they believed they used to live in or even living in a different country.

*Recognising current family members who were with them in their past life, for instance their mother in this life could have been their child in their past life. Ashley remembers being her father's mother in a previous life.

*Remembering a foreign language – sometimes a child can speak specific foreign words that have not been taught to them in their current life.

*Remembering what job they once had – one child could remember being a pilot when he lived in Germany. He has a fascination with planes in this life and has great knowledge about them even though he is very small and has not learned this from any other source. His past life recall will be seeping through because of his passion and experience of being a pilot in his previous life.

*Remembering a beloved animal from a past life. Children will say things such as I used to have a dog before in my other life.

*Remembering how they passed – these can include accidents, illnesses and even murder. They may also remember how old they were when they died. One child from India remembers being shot and killed in his past life and even remembers who did it.

*Remembering their time in the spirit world prior to their being born where they recall details of preparing their new existence. They also remember choosing their parents and the country they will live in.

There are plenty of other unique past life memories and so it is important to be open-minded and listen to and notice what your child tells you, or spontaneously mentions.

Things Children Say

Here are some of the sayings that children spontaneously come out with.

I remember when I died before
I used to have a brother/sister in my other life
I miss my other mummy and daddy
I was sick in my other life and died when I was little
I used to live in a big house with a big family
I used to be a girl/boy in my other life

I died in an accident when I was big
I used to have a dog called ....
I remember when I was big and you were little
I used to fly a plane/drive a bus/write books .... When
   I was alive before

Children have sometimes been known to speak certain words or phrases in a foreign language even though they have not been introduced to it in their current life. Some children will draw pictures of their old family or the place in which they lived or the job they used to do when they were once grown- ups. When I was little I used to sing before I could speak and the first song I ever sang was in French. Other children will draw the way in which they previously died, in a hospital bed or in an airplane crash or in a boat that is sinking and even extreme cases such as being shot. A few years ago I watched a documentary on the television about some documented cases of children's past lives in India. One such case included a young boy who remembered being shot in his past life. He could even remember who shot him and now that he was in his current life he claimed the person who shot him was still alive. The really fascinating part about this is that there was a significant birth mark on the child where he claimed to have been shot. Next you will read a story about a little boy called Harry who remembers specific details of his past life.

Harry's Story

"Harry was around five when he first mentioned to us memories of his past life. We were driving through Bath in South Wales and as we turned the car to drive down a particular road, Harry suddenly got very excited. He said, 'Mum I used to live here on this street with Grandpa when it was the war'. I was in complete shock and asked him if he was sure and he got quite upset that I did not remember. Harry was adamant he lived there but said he couldn't remember exactly which house it was but that it was during wartime. I do believe Harry was telling me the truth although I have no concrete proof but a mother knows when her child is being sincere. Harry also remembers that his name was David and that he died when he was quite young of some illness. Harry is growing up to be a very intelligent and clever young man and has kept his sensitive side. He does not remember the things he told me as a child although he believes in angels and ghosts and says that he can sometimes see them with people. I often wonder about the things he told me in childhood and inside it has given me hope that we live on somewhere after death."

Harry's mother has now become fascinated by past lives and is currently researching the spiritual pathway; she is also hoping to experience past- life regression therapy herself to find out more about her own prior existence.

Past -Life Regression

Past- life regression by an experienced and qualified practioner is a great way of experiencing past life memories. Sometimes this form of regression can bring about immense healing to a person's current lifetime if they have some kind of phobia or fear that is causing them daily problems. Past- life regression is a form of hypnotherapy that can help to induce memory recall for assessing your past lives. It is therapeutic and beneficial to those who wish to explore alternative ways in which to heal and for personal growth. Others will experience past- life regression therapy for their own curiosity in wanting to find out more about who they were before. Even with someone who is just being curious, it has the benefit of touching their soul with the knowledge that life is eternal. This can have a tremendous impact on how they conduct their life path and destiny once their eyes have been opened so to speak.

The following story is about a young girl called Angela who was fearful and anxious whenever she was near water.

Angela's Story

Angela had a terrible fear of being under water and this fear was preventing her from being comfortable enough in the water long enough for her to learn to swim. Angela's fear did not come from this lifetime as she has had no bad experiences with water and there was no rational explanation as to her distress. Angela was now 11 years old and wanted to learn to swim so she could join in with her friends who loved swimming. Eventually Angela's mum took her to see a hypnotherapist to try and locate her fear and heal it. The therapist said that sometimes people block out memories of trauma and completely forget about them although the fear connected to the memory will stay with them. Angela was placed in a light trance and slowly taken back through her childhood to try and find the source of her fear. As this continued so far without locating any trauma the therapist then asked Angela who was now in a very relaxed state, to go to the time in her life that created her fear of water.

Straight away Angela became agitated as she gasped for breath and was calling for help. The therapist calmed her down and helped her to detach from feeling the memory by having her watch it happen instead of feeling it happen. Angela was then able to tell the story of why she was afraid of water. It was because she had actually drowned in a previous existence and this trauma then carried over into her present life. Angela said that she was five years old and had gone to the lake with her sister and some other friends because it was a very hot summer's day. Angela remembers that her mother told her only to paddle in the water and not to go in any further. All the others were going further into the lake and she didn't want to look like a baby and so she ignored her mother's advice and went further in. Angela got into trouble and soon fell under the water. She remembers trying to find her way to the top but was gulping in water and soon she became confused. Suddenly she was out of the water and realised she could see her body floating face down in the water. Angela had drowned. The therapist then helped Angela to let go of this memory by performing some healing work and explaining to her subconscious that this trauma did not belong to her current life time. Angela has now faced her fears and has already taken swimming lessons in her local pool.

My Life Review

I once had a strange experience as a child when I went to the local swimming pool with my brother and our friends. I was a confident swimmer and didn't mind being under water and was playing around by touching the floor of the pool and coming up to the surface and going straight back down again. It was during a few goes of this that I became disorientated and thought that I was at the surface when in fact I was at the floor and I gulped in water by mistake. Immediately I panicked and tried to get back to the top which seemed to be impossible as I went to the side instead and became quite dizzy. Now the strange experience that happened to me was this, I had lots of flashes of different scenes and memories of my childhood that came really quickly one after the other. Next minute I reached the top and the flashes stopped. I wonder if I was reviewing my life in some way as my body and mind may have thought that I was dying. I have never forgotten that experience.

My own Regression

I was 33 years old when I experienced my first past-life regression. I did this for no other reason than I was curious and it happened to be part of my Reiki healing course. My Reiki Master, who specialised in Past-Life Regression regressed me back to a previous life time. Straight away I knew that I was a man and I also knew my name was Jack and I was around the age of twenty. I lived in England with my mother and my girlfriend and was looking for work overseas to make more money to help my family. My Reiki Master asked me to move further ahead in that life which I did and I then found out that I had travelled to New York on a big ship to find work. Apparently I had the time of my life in New York, I went out every night, I gambled by playing card games on big barrels with the other guys in the local drinking bars. I went home drunk on whiskey and beer and I smoked one after the other. I also fell madly in love with a young woman who I promised I would make her my wife. I had neglected though to mention that I had a girlfriend who lived with my mother back home in England.

My Reiki Master took me ahead six months later, I was doing a runner from my life in New York and was on a ship back to England. The only thing I left was a note to the love of my life telling her I was never coming back. I was broken- hearted but felt I had to honour my life in England. However even though I married my girlfriend and also had a son called Jack, my heart was always with my love in New York. I died in my 40's of lung cancer and with regret at not following my heart in love. After my regression I just couldn't believe how random that all sounded but the funny thing to me is that in my current life I have totally followed my heart to do with my love life and every thing else. I have also never smoked even when I was young and all my friends were trying it and I really dislike any one smoking near me. I firmly believe that we have the opportunity to overcome specific lessons when we incarnate and if we do not manage to achieve them then we have plenty of chances to have another go in a new life.

We Are Eternal Souls
Our soul will continue to have numerous experiences and different sets of life circumstances to live through. The only thing that will stay the same is the real us, our true divine spark and essence. Our soul is eternal and will continue to exist throughout many lifetimes on earth and other destinations

elsewhere. Surely you don't think that earth is the only planet where life- force energy exists? There are many options available for us to experience different levels of existence so that we can gain comparison in our valuable experiences. Our purpose is to evolve spiritually and not just as individuals but to shine a light to others who maybe haven't realised the immense joy of remembering who they really are. They are a divine spark of God with God- given gifts and creative talents to make the best of their existence and life experience. Some people may not even know that they have unlimited potential to help themselves and others too. The more we help people to remember who they are then they too start to help others and like a domino effect the light of God spreads throughout the world. An increase of God's light in the world would then help to lessen things like violence, greed, wars, poverty and other negative acts.

Dreaming of Past Lives

When I was a child I used to dream about children who were starving and living in a foreign country. The dreams were frequent and vivid and I felt that maybe I was a part of this existence at one time. I knew from my dream that the children only lived short lives and would soon go home to the spirit world. They would heal and rest and evaluate the lives they had on earth. Those who have suffered on earth in this way choose so for reasons that our conscious awareness can not or will not want to understand. All souls are amazing and they desire to gain a certain level of understanding through an array of different life themes and experiences. All spirits choose the number of years they will live and this varies from days to years so that they can fulfil their destinies. Some lives are cut short through the cruel actions of others but if this happens eventually the soul will return again to experience what they had initially set out to.

There is a Reason for Everything

There is a reason for everything, even if we cannot understand or want to understand what that may be when something goes badly wrong. When we eventually go to the spirit world we will become aware of why we have chosen to experience certain things. Many people also want to know why bad things happen to good people. A lot of people say to me that when they die they want to find out about what happened to someone who has gone missing and who was never found. This is so hard for those on earth to comprehend, especially when a child goes missing. It is human nature to want to solve the case and see if their suspicions are right and to find closure. We must not put pressure on ourselves to understand the evil in the world and to blame God for whatever has gone wrong. God does not choose to punish some people and bless others, this is not what good or bad luck is about. Man has free will and this is a gift from God and man is therefore responsible for his actions and outcomes on the earth.

Something good can come out from something bad if you just look for it and this can also be a blessing in disguise. There are many examples of this throughout the world with the courageous actions of the parents of hurt and missing children. The Amber Alert was set up in America because of this and has helped to trace and find many missing children in the early stages of their abduction.

Past Life Habits

Ask yourself this, do you or your child ever talk about wanting to visit other countries than the one you live in? Are you drawn to a particular culture, food or clothing? Do you have memories that come to you in dreams or even your day dreams, that you feel are vivid enough to mean something more to you? Have you ever yearned to visit somewhere and when you arrive there feel completely at home as if you have lived there before? Well maybe you have. I know that I am drawn to America and not just because of Disney World, which was great fun but because there is something deep inside me that makes me feel I belong there. I have plans to keep on going back to America and maybe one day even live there.

Synchronicities of Our Life Plan

As we carefully plan our lives in the spirit realm before we are ready to partake in our chosen roles in life on earth, we also set up signs and synchronicities along our way to help keep us on track. I know beyond a shadow of a doubt that a big part of my life was meant to be lived in Scotland. It was about 9 years ago that I had the most vivid dream and in my dream I was flying over the beautiful trees and the countryside of Scotland. I was accompanied by my maternal grandmother who had passed away when I was a teenager. My grandmother mentioned to me that I would soon be living in the area I could see and that I had lots to do there. The following morning I woke up knowing that in my future I would be living and working away from home. Synchronistic events soon started to unfold.

I went on a two week holiday to Scotland to visit my boyfriend and while I was there I recognised the area which I could vividly remember from my dream. This confirmed to me that I would soon live there and that this was the right path for me to take at that time. I also got another sign that it was time for me to make this big move when I received a message from a Medium in a spiritual church. The medium told me that I would soon move away to Aberdeen in Scotland and that it was the right thing to do for my career. I felt that I was being given the encouragement I needed to prepare for my life changing direction. It was to say the least, the best move I made as moving to Scotland eventually helped me find my soul- mate, now my husband and also my career as a professional psychic medium and author took off.

Since moving to Scotland I have opened a spiritual centre,

taught psychic development and healing and have written two books with a third one planned. Remember your life will flow just fine when you follow your heart, the gentle signs and synchronicities that guide your way. You have already set up some of these signs and synchronicities before you were born so that you would have signposts along your path and it is your job to be aware to notice them. When you are too busy with material world problems you can miss your signs and opportunities to move forward in your life. When this happens you may come up against many blocks and obstacles that keep you stuck until you find ways to heal your energy and realign with your spirit. In the next chapter you will read about ways in which to heal both of your vibes to create success, happiness and well-being in your lives.

Chapter Six

Healing & Manifesting

'The body is a self-healing organism, so it's really about clearing things out of the way so the body can heal itself.'
Barbara Brennan

We are Powerful Healers

Anyone can help to heal themselves if they only realise this ability lies within them. Most people even help to heal others without knowing that they do. Healing does not have to be hands on as you would expect. Healing can come from a smile, a gentle hug or touch and through words of wisdom spoken or written. Someone may say the right words needed at the right moment that will then reach the person and act as a trigger to begin their own healing. The person will then choose to ignite their spark once again and begin their own natural healing process and return back to balance and wellbeing. You may have heard of the phrases 'I am feeling low in spirit' or 'I have lost my spark' etc. wWhen this happens, the person's life force energy has dimmed and depression can set it along with physical aliments. It is important to look after your mind, body and spirit so that your energy is strong, vibrant,clean and protected. When you do take the responsibility to look after yourself, then you are preventing emotional, mental and physical ailments from manifesting. It is wise to teach your children to look after their energies so that they learn from a young age how to heal themselves. At the end of this chapter there will be a healing exercise to help clean out your aura so that you can remove any negative energy. This exercise will help both you and your child to feel great benefit in your overall health and wellbeing.

Reiki Healing

A healer is a channel that attracts healing energies to pass through them and then into the person needing the healing. No one can heal anyone else though as they are not responsible for other people's thoughts, actions and emotions. You can only heal yourself but this does not mean that you cannot have a hand in helping a person to have the courage to do so. As a Reiki Master/Teacher I am a channel for healing energies to pass through me and to the person needing healing. I do not do the healing myself, I just act as the channel so that the healing from the universe can ground through me and to my client.

If you are interested in becoming a Reiki Healer then you need to find a recommended Reiki Master. They will then give you an attunement to the Reiki healing so that a channel is opened for the healing to pass through. The healing then enters into the client's mind, body and spirit and goes to wherever is needed for their highest good. Children can be attuned to Reiki so that they can channel healing energies to themselves, their loved ones and even their pets. Becoming attuned to Reiki healing will help both you and your child to raise your vibration. The more vibrant and light your vibration becomes then you will attract better health and happiness towards you.

Intention to Heal

Healing can be performed by anyone who has a desire and the intention to help heal another. When this desire comes from a place of compassion and empathy with a true intent to help another, then healing energies will be attracted to the person. When this happens there may be warmth and a tingling sensation in the hands along with a desire to place the hands on the person to give healing. Healing in this way is coming from Spirit through Spirit to Spirit without the process of attunement.

The main purpose of healing is to touch the soul to the fact that it is eternal and therefore has the ability to heal itself.

Healing can also be sent to others through prayer or a request for healing energies to help someone in need. Maybe your loved one is on the other side of the world and distance will not get in the way of the healing energies reaching someone in an instant. The power of prayer is mighty - remember you can ask Archangel Raphael the healing angel to give healing to any of your loved ones or friends. You can also imagine your loved one surrounded in a beautiful green healing light. Healing offers the person unconditional love and assistance within their daily lives and wherever it is needed for them.

Vibration

The environment in which you live along with other family members, who live with you will have an effect on your vibration. The effect can be both positive and negative depending on the energy vibrations that are being unconsciously absorbed. For instance any negative vibrations that stem from an argument by family members will linger in the room long after the argument has finished. Psychic children are extra- sensitive and your child will absorb these feelings which can make them feel off -balance and out of sorts. They will be tuning into and picking up on the low vibes caused by others. Do not be fooled into thinking that this is not as bad as it sounds as just because we cannot see energy vibrations with our physical eyes, does not mean that they are not still there. In fact they can linger on for days and weeks if the arguments are passionate and particularly heated.

The Home Environment

It is important to create a happy and healthy home for the care and well-being of both you and your child. Your home environment has a direct effect on your overall energy and if it is not a happy healthy place to dwell then it is going to have some negative effect on your state of health. Things that can make an environment drain your life force energy will be as follows –

Family arguments
A cluttered unloved home
Lack of light in the home
Noise interruptions
No garden
No routine for meal times

These examples are just some of the ways in which any of the family's energies can be affected. There are ways in which you can change these things to create a much brighter, faster and lighter vibration for your home. Even making small subtle changes will eventually help you to notice the amazing difference in your own energy and the way other people in your family interact more positively.

The steps you can take to counteract the low vibes are as follows –

Family arguments – never go to bed on a disagreement - learn how to communicate all of your needs properly without turning to anger. Honour and respect the needs of the entire household as children need to be heard. If there have been heated arguments then there will be energetic anger in the air and this needs to be cleared. Low vibes can be easily absorbed by others in the family and then you find you will have a family of angry people. To clear the bad air you can open all the windows and let the air in. Use incense and waft it around the rooms, especially the one the arguments took place in. Play some beautiful music. Sort out your differences. All of the above will then help to dissolve the negative vibes.

A cluttered unloved home – a cluttered house is a cluttered mind and a life that can be drained of valuable life- force energy. If you are having problems sleeping or you suffer from headaches and feel stuck in your life then maybe there is a need to de-clutter. Make sure that all of the corners in every room of your home are clear of clutter so that the new vibrant energy that is about to come in can circulate around your home. When you let go of the old you prepare for the new, you will feel lighter in mind, body and spirit once you have sorted out your entire home. Try and find creative ways in which to make your home pretty, welcoming and comfortable to you all. When you love your home you will love to keep it clean and tidy and this will also reflect the love you have for yourself and everyone else in your household. Notice how much you have raised the vibration of your home as you notice how everyone one in it feels a lot happier.

A lack of light in the home – it is important to let your house bathe in as much natural light as possible during the day. To do this make sure you open all curtains and blinds and let that light shine through. Clean the windows if they are dirty so that the light can sparkle through and open the windows to let fresh sunlight in. If parts of your home are dark and you are not able to direct natural light there then you can use artificial light by placing a lamp to light up the darkness. Again if you find it difficult to let natural light flow into your home ,then another way to help lighten the vibration can be through choosing light colours to paint your walls such as white etc. You can also light candles but make sure you remember to blow out the flame before you go out or to bed. It is important to keep your home as vibrant as possible.

Noise interruptions – if your child needs quiet time to do their homework, make sure they have their own special place where this is possible, even if it is their bedroom. It is very important to have quiet time and somewhere to go for any family members to have time to themselves if they choose so. Turn off the television if you are not actually focussed on it as this will stop you from connecting to your higher self by acting as a distraction. Notice if there are any other noise distractions in your life that you can directly stop. It is very important to have quite time so that you connect with God and your higher self. In doing this you can gain insight into what you need to do next in your life and how best to do so. Remember the answers are within you and for you to hear them then you need some quiet reflection. Taking time to meditate will help you to connect with your soul.

If you have noisy neighbours and have simply tried everything you can do about the situation and it does not get any better, then you really need to move home. If you feel that you are trapped there and this is just not possible to move home because of money issues or anything else that you feel is blocking you, then you need to hand it over to the universe for help. Ask for guidance and trust that you will be helped to move forward then notice the signs so that you can take action. Nothing is impossible and miracles do happen and you do not need to know how they happen; all you need is to be open to them. Create the best vibration in your home first so that you will begin to attract the move you so desire.

No garden – it is important to get some outdoor time and connect with nature. When you are feeling stressed there is nothing better than going outside to connect with nature even if it is just being in your garden. Taking a walk amongst the greenery of the countryside or park or along the beach front will do you the world of good. In other words do not let the fact that you have no garden stop you from finding the time to get some valuable fresh air and beautiful scenery. When you walk amongst nature you are cleansing your aura, bringing clarity to your mind and energising the body and soul. If you have been worrying about a problem you may find that the solution will just pop into your mind during your walk. Your physical body needs exercise to keep it subtle and movement will help your vibration to circulate around your body keeping it strong and healthy.

When you go outside you ground your energy to the earth and grounding your energy can help to centre you in the present moment. This can help you become less scattered and weary and more focussed and energised. If you feel particularly stressed or annoyed or your child is upset or sulky then go outdoors and jump and up down to ground your energy to the earth. If you can, it is also great to feel the earth or grass underneath your bare feet. If you cannot leave your house for whatever reason then maybe you can go for a walk in your neighbourhood or the very least sit near an open window. Your spirit needs to be energised and one of the best ways to feed your soul is to connect with nature, fresh air and exercise.

No routine for meal times – it is important as a family to eat together and if possible to eat around the dinner table. This not only helps the family to connect with each other as a group but also it is valuable for them to feel they are being looked after, cared for and nurtured. When you eat together you connect together and this is when you can share aspects of your day or offer support for anyone who is feeling low or who is going through some disappointment. The backing of the family unit will help each member to feel emotionally supported so that they have the strength and unconditional love to move forward. Sometimes it is difficult to eat together because of everyone's different schedules but compromise together and you will all be able to work something out. It is also important whenever possible to have home- cooked food with plenty of fresh fruit and vegetables. They offer more life -giving energy to your body than that of processed food that is full of additives, preservatives and colourings. Drink plenty of water to help your energy flow around your body and keep you hydrated. We are what we eat and it is your responsibility to teach your child to eat well and be healthy. All of these steps can lead to you strengthening your aura.

Children & Auras

Some children are particularly drawn towards beautiful colours and love to draw other people with lots of colours around them. If you have a child who likes to do this, then what they are actually doing is clairvoyantly tuning into someone's aura because they see or sense the colours that are around them. By learning more about colours and their energy vibrations, you will discover a wealth of knowledge about a person's health, personality and nature. Read on to find out more about what your favourite colour says about you both and also what colours to surround yourself with to heal your vibes or to manifest specific qualities.

Colours of the Soul

*Red – this colour is the colour of ambition, courage, passion and security in life. If either of you like this colour then you will be serious about what you put your heart and soul into and will like to do well. You will want to feel safe and secure in your life and need to feel supported by those you trust and love. You will not like to fail at anything and can be quite sensitive if you are second best or lose in something. You can be quite hard on yourselves to succeed but when you do, you are overwhelmed with happiness and this will stir you on to do something new.

If you or your child is tired and fatigued then red is a great colour for you both to wear as it helps to energise your vibrations.

*Orange – this colour is the colour of creative passion and new beginnings. If you or your child really likes this colour then you will both be creative and enjoy things such as reading, writing, drawing and painting amongst other creative talents such as singing and dancing. You will also enjoy exercise and sporting activity and will enjoy the outdoors and nature. Maybe you both have a talent for poetry or you are equally good at coming up with new ideas and inspirations. You can both be extra- sensitive and sometimes teary- eyed when you feel out of sorts. Keep a journal of your thoughts and feelings as you may come up with something quite unique. Also when you are extra-sensitive, then writing down your feelings will help to clear them away from your mind so that when you go to bed you have no trouble sleeping. So many people have insomnia as they find it difficult to switch off from their troubles and concerns. Peace of mind will bring you a peaceful sleep and when you are sleeping your body is regenerating itself and healing. Teach your child to get their feelings down on paper and they will release the pressure from their mind and give themselves a chance to heal.

If you or your child are feeling low in emotions and stuck in some way, then orange is a great colour to wear to help balance and shift the low vibes so that you are back in your creative flow.

*Yellow – this is the colour of confidence, willpower and study. If you or your child likes this particular colour then you will both have a happy- go-lucky and bubbly personality. You will like to learn lots of new things and want to study so that you gain knowledge and wisdom to move ahead in your life. Your sunny disposition will help you both to attract fun friends and happiness in your life. You will have a strong character and will be determined and able to speak your mind and stand up for yourself. Sometimes you may be too quick in making a decision because you didn't check in with your intuition and listened to your ego instead. This can happen if you are over-excitable or nervous. You may also be indecisive on times and when you become stressed you may have a sore stomach. Yellow is a beautiful colour to include in your home as it can lift your spirits and bring inspiration to you to make a positive change. You will love to travel and in your future you will feel the urge to travel more. You will be drawn to overseas as well as to your own country.

If you and your child are feeling nervous, then surround yourself with the colour yellow. It will help you to become more confident and strong- minded. This is also a good colour to have around you when you are studying or researching something. So yellow is a great colour for children to wear when they do their homework.

*Green – this colour is the colour of peace, harmony, unconditional love and balance. If you or your child likes this particular colour then you will be drawn to help others by your very kind- hearted nature. You can sometimes become worn out as you give too much of your energy to others without realising that you are being drained. There is a need to set boundaries as being so caring can lead others to manipulate you as you don't like to say no to them. In fact you may need to focus on creating balance in your life so that you have work, rest and play and not too much of one and not enough of the others etc. You will be able to forgive but not forget as words can hurt you and stay with you. Your child may be interested in becoming a doctor, nurse or vet or some kind of healer as this colour is connected to the healing vibration.

If either of you feel like you are out of balance and are not having quality time to yourselves, then green is the colour to wear to help bring you peace and harmony within. If you are scattered with your emotions and are angry or stressed then this is a great colour to surround yourself with.

*Pink – this colour is the colour of the psychic senses and unconditional love. It is a very feminine energy but this doesn't stop any males from liking it. If you or your child likes this particular colour then you will be extra- sensitive to the energies around you. This psychic ability will be expressed through the gift of clairsentience where you feel others' emotional pain and have compassion for them. This is the colour of love and the love that unites family as well as your love- life. You will wear your hearts on your sleeves as you will express your love outwards to others. You will both be romantic in nature and will want to feel number one to those who love you including your best friends. You will like to be hugged and kissed by those you love to help you feel safe and secure and nurtured. You will love to have nice things around you and you will be sensitive about the way you look. Sometimes you may be too self-critical and may need to be more unconditional towards yourself and accept who you are. You will have amazing imaginations and love to day- dream. You will also love to watch romantic comedies and funny films as they feed your soul.

If you both need to love yourself a little more, then pink is a great colour to wear. Again pink is a loving healing vibration that can help you accept yourself.

*Turquoise Blue – this colour is the colour of self-expression and truth. If you or your child likes this particular colour, then you will be drawn to living your truth by trusting in your feelings and intuition, and going with the heart and not the false trappings of the ego. This colour is the colour of confidence, healing, knowledge and wisdom. You will be drawn to the path of study and then put what you have learned to practice.

If either you or your child needs to become confident to speak up for yourselves then this is a brilliant colour to wear. If your child is nervous about speaking in front of an audience during their school play then this is a great colour for them to have under their school uniform. If you or your child would like to learn a new language then this is a great colour to surround yourself with.

*Indigo – this colour is the colour of dreaming of the future and your life- path destiny. If you or your child likes this particular colour then you will have a great imagination. You have specific dreams and goals about the future that you eventually want to happen. You will have a clear intention of what you want from your life and will aspire to make the changes or take the chances you need to fulfil your destiny. If either of you have picked this colour you will display clair-voyant abilities or have psychic dreams and predictions that you will sometimes remember in your waking life.

If you or your child has sore eyes or headaches, then this dark and velvet indigo colour will help to induce healing and relieve any blockages in your energy fields.

*Violet – this is the colour of your connection with the Divine or what I know as God. If you or your child likes this particular colour then you will have a strong faith in yourself, your life and have faith in God. You will believe in a higher power that is guiding and healing you along your life path. Your child will know that they are from Heaven and you will both be aware that you have some psychic abilities. You may both have the awareness of spirits around you and be sensitive to the gift of mediumship.

If you or your child feels lonely or feel that you have obstacles in your path, then this is the colour to wear or surround yourself with. Ask and it is given. Heaven's help is all around you.

How to heal your Aura

Our aura consists of subtle colour vibrations that will change colour and shape as a direct result of our thoughts, feelings and emotions. When we are emotionally and mentally strong our vibes will reflect this and our physical body will be in good health. When we are depressed, angry and emotionally or mentally drained, then our vibes will also reflect this and our physical body will be out of sorts and lacking in valuable life force energy to maintain itself. This can then cause physical aches and pains or even the beginning stages of an illness or depression. As we are energetic beings we are easily influenced by the energies of other people and also the environment in which we live or visit. To finish this chapter I will include an exercise that will help both you and your child to clean away any absorbed energies that do not belong to you and then you will be able to call back your own energy into the present moment so that it is strong, healthy and vibrant and you will be ready to manifest your dreams and desires.

Exercise To Heal Your Vibes

This exercise will help you to clean your energy and rid yourself of any foreign 'energies' you may have unwittingly absorbed. Also it will help to bring back all of your own energy if others have unconsciously taken it so that you are running at the best vibration you can achieve at this moment in time. Once you have finished this exercise you will be one step closer to manifesting your hearts desires. Find yourself a comfy seat and make sure you allow at least five minutes where you will not be disturbed. This is your chance to make a difference in your health and your life.

Grounding Healing Exercise

As you are an energetic being you will need to ground your energy so that you are not overwhelmed with the daily pressures of life and therefore become off- balance. You are going to be using the gravity of the Earth to help pull out any absorbed foreign energies that are not serving your highest good. Place your attention on the base of your spine and imagine that you are forming a wide hollow trunk that is about to be sucked deep into the earth. Give this trunk a particular colour: this is your grounding cord and you are now going to demand to yourself that any foreign energies or negative absorbed energies now leave you via this cord and travel deep into the earth. *Note;* the earth will not be affected by these energies as they will be neutralised and disintegrated. Now imagine yourself dropping this grounding cord into the earth and then place a bubble of white sparkly light around you, under your feet and over your head just like a cocoon.

Now it's time to call back your energy from the past, present and future. These may be where your worries are focussed or stuck. Also if anyone else is unconsciously taking your energy ,then now it is time to retrieve it as at the end of the day it is yours. You need all of your energy to create and manifest good health, dreams and the fulfilment of your desires. Think of your favourite colour: let's say you have chosen pink. As you cannot see your life force energy you have now given it a specific colour so that it will become easy to visualise it coming back to you. Now I want you to tell yourself that you would now like all of your life force energy to come back to you where it belongs.

This energy can come from many different areas, time - frames and people, so give your self a few minutes to imagine this particular exercise. As your pink energy is about to be absorbed back into you, see it first enter a huge bright beautiful sun that you have placed right in front of you. This will act like a healing filter that will clean your energy and make it especially vibrant ready to rejoin you. Once you have finished this exercise, smile and know that you have just made an energetic effort to make positive changes in your life. See yourself surrounded by a beautiful white light, again in the shape of a cocoon and now you can get on with the rest of the day. I wish you happy vibes for success, love and well-being and manifesting your desires.

Chapter Seven

Ghosts, Spirits & Afraid of the Dark

'I've always seen the bright lights of the angels, and I know that lower-entities can't disguise this light, because it only comes from the Love of God .'
Doreen Virtue

Ghosts

Children's encounters with ghosts are more frequent than you can imagine and you will read about some of their real- life stories in this chapter. Psychic children are able to interact with and talk to ghosts and even help them to cross over to the other side. Ghosts really do exist and you will soon find out what you need to do should you come across a meddling one. Some ghosts are helpful and others can be full of mischief. The one thing that all these ghosts have in common, though, is that they are earthbound. Earthbound spirits have simply chosen to stay connected to the earth after they have died for their own individual reasons. Such reasons can be to stay close to a loved one or to stay attached to their beloved home, pets or material possessions and even money.

You may wonder why a ghost would want to stay attached to their money as they are unable to spend it now that they have died. It is because they firmly believe it still belongs to them and they want to know what is going to happen to it. These kinds of ghosts would be very material in life and become greedy with the accumulation of their lifetime finances and accomplish-ments. Other reasons ghosts choose to hang around the earth are because of their addiction to drink or drugs and so they choose to hang around those who have the same kind of addictions. This is because they are able to attach to the living person's energy field to actually receive the feeling once again of being drunk or high on drugs.

Ghosts can also become trapped to the Earth plane dimension because they have missed their chance to cross over to the light and remain stuck where they are. This can happen because they ignore the time frame they have to cross into the light and then find that they are stuck. These wandering ghosts can become confused as time passes them by without them even realising it. All ghosts eventually return to the spirit world and there are numerous spirit helpers to guide them over when they are ready but remember ghosts have free will and cannot be forced to cross over. When someone dies their physical body ceases to exist in this world but their spirit moves on to the spirit world. Only those spirits who decide to stay behind or get stuck become earthbound ghosts. For the multitude of spirits who do cross over to the light they will find themselves reunited once again with their loved ones who have passed before them. Spirits who have crossed over are also able to visit us on earth and then return back to spirit when they so desire. It is because of this significance that I will call these 'visiting spirits' and not earth-bound spirits.

Sharing your House with a Ghost

One thing you need to be aware of if you are sharing your house with a ghost is that they need to tap into an energy source to be able to stay active. This energy source can even come from you or your child and this can leave both of you feeling tired, drained or depleted in energy. It is not wise to let a ghost live amongst the family unit even if the ghost seems to be pleasant enough. First of all it is not fair for the ghost as they would be much better off crossing over into the light of the spirit world whether they are aware of this or not. Secondly other problems can manifest in your home because of your ghostly lodger such as electrical problems, heating and plumbing problems.

You may also have problems with constant sickness, with one illness after the other and things just not going right in your life. Light bulbs can be used up quickly or even flash on and off and the television can work on its own without the remote control. If you feel that the energy in the house is low and depressive or even has a heavy feeling to it along with the other signs and symptoms mentioned, then you may have a ghost abiding with you. Some ghosts are easily noticed by children who may then befriend them and have them as their so called imaginary friend. Imaginary friends can be earthbound spirits or visiting spirits. It is much better if the child is friends with a visiting spirit.

Imaginary Friends

The following stories are about two children who had imaginary friends - one was with an earthbound ghost and the other one with a visiting spirit.

Katie's Story

Katie was around the age of three when she started talking to her imaginary friend a little spirit boy called 'Soley'. At first Katie's mum thought it was just her imagination but she had never heard of such a name as Soley before and asked Katie how she knew such an unusual name. Katie said she asked her friend what his name was and he said it was Soley. Katie's mum was intrigued and decided to look up the unusual name on the internet. What she found was – it was a Latin boy's name and the meaning of the name was 'Sun' and less than 150 babies born in the USA has this name. Katie explained to her mum that Soley didn't live with them because he lived in Heaven but he visited her when he could because he liked to play games with her.

The games included singing and dancing and playing with her toys in her room. Her mum often noticed Katie talking into thin air as if she was having a proper conversation with someone that wasn't there. Once she even mentioned that Soley was in the car with them as he wanted to go to the seaside also. Katie carried on talking and playing with her spirit friend up until the age of six when her mum noticed that it became less frequent. When her mother asked Katie if she still spoke to Soley Katie explained that he was busy in school and was not able to visit her as much.

Katie's story offers clues that her spirit friend Soley was in fact a visiting spirit and not a ghost. The clues include the fact that he wasn't always around Katie as he used to come and go again. Soley also told Katie that he didn't live with her because he lived in Heaven. The other clue is that around the age of six the visits became less frequent. Many children have these kinds of imaginary friends, the spirit children often have lots in common with the psychic children and this is why they are attracted to them as friends. There is nothing wrong with this kind of spirit friend because the spirit is from the light and will not drain or cause any kind of worry or fear to the psychic child. The spirit may also be the psychic child's friend from back home and they want to stay in touch with them until it is their time to incarnate to earth. The next story is about a spirit friend who was in fact an earthbound spirit child.

Sarah's Story

Sarah was five years old and lived with her parents and brother in an old Victorian home. Sarah soon complained to her mother that she could here noises in the house and was afraid to go to bed at night because she thought that someone was in her room. One day Sarah told her mother that she saw a little ghost girl who was dressed funny and the little ghost girl told Sarah that she lived in her house and was looking for her mummy. Sarah's mum wasn't sure what to do about this information but wanted to help her stop feeling scared of being in her own home. Sarah's mother called in a medium to see if they could make contact with the child. The medium soon found out that the child had died in a house- fire many years before and had not crossed over because she stayed behind to look for her family. The medium explained that visiting spirits had been trying to help her cross over but she was so fixed to the earth plane dimension to look for her parents that she couldn't see or hear their help. The medium gently told the little ghost child that she had died and needed to go to the light as her mummy was waiting to see her again. This time the child took notice and with the help from the medium the spirit child went to Heaven.

The little ghost child was an earthbound spirit as she was living in Sarah's house all the time instead of visiting now and again. She was also full of sadness and stuck in her endless search for her parents who had already crossed over. Earthbound spirits appear to be more solid to those who are able to see them and this is another way they are different from visiting spirits who will be shimmering and transparent when seen. The little ghost- child's free will had stopped her from receiving help and guidance from the spirit world as she refused to leave the home she knew. The little ghost would need to sustain her energy force to be active on the earth plane and so she focused on someone from the family who now lived in her old home. The fearful emotions emitted from Sarah would have helped the little ghost- child to use the energy vibrations from her aura to sustain her.

She would have also been lonely and in need of a friend and would have chosen Sarah as a playmate. Other family members may have also been affected with illness such as colds, flu or skin irritations and there would have been a depressive heavy energy within the household due to the fact that there was an unhappy ghost. Read below for an exercise to help an unhappy ghost cross over to the spirit world. You do not need a medium to do this but if you would prefer to use one then make sure that they come recommended. In other words you do not want a cowboy medium that will be of no help at all and may cause you more fear along with charging you a hefty fee. I know there are such people out there who would do this.

Exercise to help an Unhappy Ghost go back home

Go to the room where you feel the unhappy ghost frequents the most or where you have seen the ghost. Address the ghost by speaking aloud and telling them that you are able to help them go back home to Heaven where their loved ones are waiting for them. Now silently ask your guardian angel to help you help this earthbound spirit to go back home. Next ask your angel to help bring the light that is the doorway to the spirit world. Imagine this light is in the room - you can focus it on a particular wall and instruct the earthbound spirit to notice this light that goes beyond the confines of the room. Tell them that when they walk into this light their loved ones will be waiting for them and that they will be safe and happy once again. If they are hesitant or do not trust you as they may think you are trying to trick them, ask your angel to help bring the earthbound's spirit family as near as possible so that the earthbound may see them and follow them into the light. Remember to be gentle as the earthbound can be confused or even afraid to believe you. Hopefully the earthbound will take this opportunity to move on and go back home. Thank your angel and see the light close up until it becomes a pinpoint in the distance and then eventually disappears.

You will soon know if the earthbound spirit has crossed over as the atmosphere in the household will lift and feel lighter and more vibrant. Also any noises or other disturbances will totally stop and your child will no longer feel fearful in their own home. If the earthbound spirit refuses to leave or you feel you have not helped them to cross over then you should enlist the help of a rescue medium. Sometimes children are afraid of the dark and of going to bed at night as they think there is someone in their room with them. If this is the case there are ways in which you can help them to ease their fears.

Afraid of the Dark

When children think of ghosts they think of them appearing to them at night when it is dark. This can create all kinds of fear related to sleep and bedtime. When I was little I remember being afraid of the dark and bedtime as I always heard other- worldly voices talking in my room. Any noise or disturbance when the lights were out always seemed to be much more intense than they actually were. If your child has the same kind of fears then there are a few things that you can do to help them. First you need to listen to what they are actually afraid of.

Ashley was two years old and having problems sleeping through the night. She told her mum that a lady was in her room talking to her. Her mum was woken up every single night with Ashley crying that a woman was in her room. Ashley's mum was so tired herself that she decided to address the spirit by telling her that her visits were waking Ashley up and disturbing everyone's sleep and that she has to stop doing this. The following evening Ashley slept soundly for the first time and her mum was relieved that she followed her instincts and took action.

Remember that you or your child are always in control and can tell the spirit that they are not to come near and frighten you at nighttime. A visiting spirit may not intend to do this and will listen to you. An earthbound spirit may carry on interfering but remember you have been given the exercise to help them cross over. If your child is afraid of the dark even though there are no disturbances from ghostly visitors, then you can place a rose quartz crystal at the side of their bed. This healing stone will help to ease their fears. Tell them it is a special healing stone that will help to protect them when they are sleeping. You can also tell them they have a special guardian angel who won't let anything hurt them and that they can choose a name for their angel and ask their angel to help them sleep and not be afraid. In fact you can even ask your child's guardian angel on their behalf to step in and help them settle during the night. Next read about other experiences that your child may have during their sleep.

Children who Astral Travel

As a child I had the experience of astral travelling which meant leaving my body during sleep to visit the spirit realms and other spirits also on their travels. Everyone who falls into a deep sleep will at some time temporarily leave their bodies and go on an astral visit, although this will be done unconsciously. Visits can include meeting up with loved ones who have already passed on – this is especially good for parents who are grieving the loss of their child as they are able to reconnect once again. On waking up you may have some kind of memory of your visit and think it was only a dream but your soul fully remembers this encounter and this helps with the grieving process.

Sometimes you or your child may get a feeling of *déjà vu* which is the feeling you get when you think you have been to a place before because you somehow recognise it. The thing is, though you know that you have never actually been there your spirit has and may have checked out the place prior to you going there. Flying in a dream is often a sign that you are on your astral travels. Psychic children can have very vivid dreams and this can often be portrayed by their parents as an over -active imagination. Listen to what your children tell you about their dreams as it can give you a clue to what they have been up too on their astral visits. Have you or your child ever felt really light-headed just before you fell asleep? If so you may actually be aware of the beginning stages of your astral travel.

I remember trying to fall asleep before I would actually leave my body as I knew what was about to happen to me and I did not like it. It started with a funny feeling inside me and then it felt that all of me was expanding in my head area and that I was about to pop out of my head. My head felt so much bigger than it actually was and I had no feeling in the rest of my body. I can only describe it now as my whole consciousness fitting into my head ready to exit to visit the spirit realms. Sometimes on waking up I could remember vivid details about visiting with my loved ones who had already died and it felt so real to me. If you are worried about having these feelings then you need to ask your guardian angel to stop this from happening to you while you are awake. There is nothing to fear during your sleep as you are quite happy to travel around while your body is in healing mode. Next we look at children who have nightmares or night terrors.

Nightmares, Night Terrors & Catalepsy

I have had experiences with nightmares and catalepsy and a relative of mind has experienced night terrors. Nightmares usually express your fears and insecurities from problems in your waking life and if you face these problems and deal with them then the nightmares will eventually stop. If they are recurring nightmares then this is a major sign of stress and fear with something in your waking life that needs to be addressed as soon as you can. You do this by looking directly at what the recurring theme is – for instance when I was a child I had a recurring nightmare about a strange man trying to catch me. I used to run away and he chased after me and then I would fall or my knees would buckle and give in. I would then feel him grab me and I would wake up in a cold sweat.

The start of these recurring nightmares was at the time when the head teacher at my school gave an emergency assembly to discuss the need for us to be careful of strangers as there had been a strange man seen hanging around the school. I remember the teacher saying that the man had been noticed driving a white car and that we were not to approach any strangers, especially in a white car. I was a very sensitive child and this affected me deeply, it was the first time that I felt a fear of the outside world and it hit me that not everyone was a good person. It was because of this shock to my nervous system that all of my fears exploded in my dreams.

At the time I didn't know how to deal with the nightmares I had. My mother was always there for me when I needed her during the night and this definitely helped me as she did make me feel safe. It was in the outside world that I felt unsafe in. Now I know how to deal with nightmares and if your child is having recurring nightmares there are a couple of things that you can do to help them. First they need reassurance that they are safe and well. Their nightmares may include them or you being hurt in some way. This is a fear of death and of being harmed and so there is a need to let them know that it was only their fears playing out in a dream.

Find out about what their dream is about and see if you can notice if any of it fits in with what is happening in their young life. Maybe they have seen a programme on the television that scared them or it can be something like what happened to me when my teacher told me about the stranger. At the end of the day it can be a number of things that has caused the nightmares but, with a process of illumination, you can find out what it is. My issues were to do with trust and naivety as I must have viewed everyone else in the world as good people. This can be overwhelming to a sensitive child to discover that there are evil people out there who would hurt a child.

Another powerful thing you can do to help your child put their mind at rest is to address them during their deep sleep. Sit beside them and quietly talk and tell them that they are safe and secure and that they are protected by God. These words will go into their subconscious mind and help to change the old memories of fear into ones of peace. You may be inspired to know exactly what to say to help your child release their fears and if so trust that you are being guided. Your child will soon grow out of their fears and insecurities and their nightmares will cease. I do know that if children are very sensitive they will worry about things happening more so than other children and so patience may be needed.

Sensitive children get clingy and fearful when they are aware of the fact that the world is not only full of good people but there are bad ones as well. Let them know this is true as telling the truth is always the best option. Let them know that they are good and so they will only attract good people to them. This is the spiritual law of like attracts like. Teach them the power of their intuition as this is the power of discernment. If they feel unhappy or uncomfortable around any person ,then they need to trust their feelings and leave immediately or find someone they do trust and ask for help.

Night Terrors

Has your child ever experienced what is known as night terrors? They mainly affect younger children and occur more with boys than with girls. Night terrors are periods of extreme agitation with manifestations of intense fear, crying and screaming during sleep. When a child has a night terror waking them can be difficult. He or she may have their eyes open but will look straight through you, similar to someone sleepwalking. They will not be able to recall the incident in the following morning. By the age of 8 years old, half the cases will have grown out of this but about a third will carry on into adolescence. Although the exact cause of night terrors is unknown, they are most commonly triggered by being over- tired. Sometimes no treatment is necessary expect for a bedtime schedule that ensures proper sleep. A good bedtime routine is important for a child to have enough sleep so that they are fully energised for the coming day.

Night terrors are generally infrequent and usually stop on

their own without specific treatment. If your child has an attack at a certain time after they go to sleep then often the disturbance of their sleep pattern approximately fifteen minutes beforehand will prevent them from having an attack that night. You need to gently wake them before their attack would usually happen and then let them fall back to sleep and this should be repeated each night. If the above methods don't help and the attacks are violent, talk to your doctor about possible medication.

Catalepsy

I have had quite scary experiences with what is known as catalepsy. With my experiences I am aware that my mind has woken up before my body has and that I cannot physically move but I can see and hear clearly. This is very frightening as you feel that you are literally paralysed with fear but your other senses are alert and you aware that you are trapped. I first experienced this after divorce from my first marriage, probably because of emotional distress. When I had been through a period of healing the experiences stopped but they returned once again when I made a big decision to move from my home to Scotland. Again this was until I found myself settled and safe and secure and they left as quickly as they appeared. I believe that emotional stress was the trigger that brought on my outbursts. The way in which I managed to deal with the frightening episodes when they began was to try and remain as calm as I could and mentally tell myself that I would soon wake up and it would pass. I also took steps in my waking life to acknowledge my insecurities and fears so that I could sleep well and deeply. The last thing I did was to make sure I had a night- time routine. If you or your child has the same kind of experiences, then these steps will help you to overcome them. Remember there are sleep specialists that are able to offer you further assistance if you need it. To finish this chapter I will leave you with some real- life stories of children's encounters with visiting spirits.

Spirit Encounters

Around the age of five, I found myself communicating with a spirit child. I seemed to be able to know information about this spirit without her talking to me aloud. I knew she was a girl and I knew she was around my age although I could only see her as a vibrating shimmer of light in the shape of a body but I felt everything else about her. I remember thinking how great it was that I could feel her energy force. I kept pushing my hand to hers and then having a feeling and pressure push back. She communicated to me by my thoughts and I remember her giggling when I pushed my hands to her hands. I told my father who was passing by what I could feel but my father assumed it was my imagination, smiled and carried on by. The spirit child was a visiting spirit who had passed to the light when she was a baby and was visiting with me because we had our age in common. Visiting spirits have a wonderful glow about them which is transparent and shimmering if you are lucky enough to catch a glimpse of them.

Kylie's Spirit Encounter

Kylie had a visit from the spirit of her great- grandmother who wanted to pass on a message of support to Kylie's mother. Kylie has always been extremely sensitive and would pick up psychic information about her family if anyone was upset or ill. Kylie also spoke to spirits as they sometimes visited with her to pass on their messages. One morning Kylie awoke to tell her mother that some lady called Margaret came to see her as she wanted her to pass on a message to her mum from her. Margaret was in fact her mother's grandmother and this made her mum really pleased to know that her beloved grandmother had come to visit.

Margaret wanted to tell Kylie's mum that soon her father would need to go to hospital because he would become ill but he would be ok again so she must not be too worried. Kylie's mum was a bit concerned with the message because he dad was not ill at all and seemed to be quite fit and healthy. One week later though, her father got admitted to hospital with kidney failure. Kylie told her mum to remember the message off Margaret and it was because of this they felt that he would pull through and be ok again. After initially a period of no improvement, the Doctor soon noticed signs that her dad was responding to treatment and he was on the mend. Kylie and her mother have no doubt in their minds that Margaret came to reassure them that he would be ok. Kylie has a special gift that is able to reach out and help others and maybe she will be drawn to the psychic, healing or mediumship pathway in her future.

Sheila's Spirit Encounter

Sheila was twelve years old and lived with her parents and grandmother in their farmhouse in the country. Sheila was very close to her grandmother and loved her dearly but one day Sheila happened to say something cheeky to her and was told off by her Dad for doing this. This just happened to be the last day that Sheila ever saw her grandmother alive again as during that day she took a turn for the worse and passed away. Sheila was devastated and especially as she had been cheeky the last time she had spoken to her. After her grandmother's death, Sheila cried herself to sleep nearly every night and just couldn't shake off the feeling of guilt and grieving. One particular night Sheila started to see a light build up slowly at the end of her bed and in the centre of this light she could see her grandmother's smiling face. Her grandmother waved at her and told her that she was ok and loved her. This was exactly what Sheila needed to ease her grief and begin her path of healing. Immediately after this visit Sheila felt lighter in spirit and never cried at night because of what happened ever again.

What a beautiful connection between grandmother and granddaughter, Sheila's grandmother knew that Sheila was suffering and wanted to help her to let go of her pain and move on. This story can also be used as an example to us when we think of what we do or say to others as no- one can know if it will be the last words they hear. Take time in your life to let your loved ones know how special they are and never go away on an argument.

The next and final chapter is to help you with the care and nurturing of your psychic child.

Chapter Eight

Spiritual Guidance for You and Your Child

'Train up a child in the way he should go,
And when he is old he will not depart from it. '
Proverbs 22:6 King James Version

Encouragement

Children who have a positive and happy childhood receive the gifts and tools needed to help them live life as an adult and survive in the world when the going gets tough. These gifts are those of unconditional love and encouragement in the creativity of the child. This support from the parents will help the child to develop self-belief, self-love and a strong sense of self, forming a well-developed personality. For the utmost success and harmony in the life of the child, they would also need to incorporate the use of their sixth sense and intuition. It is never too late to learn about their spiritual side as by doing so will help to bring about a deep sense of meaning and understanding within. Parents who are aware of who they really are can then help the child to be aware of their own sixth sense and intuition so that they can rely on their feelings throughout their lives.

Parents are their children's guides in the early stages of their life until the time comes for the child to take responsibility to live their own path and destiny. An awareness of their sixth sense along with the unconditional love and encouragement received during a child's early years will mean that they will have a good grounding. This grounding will help them to be ready to achieve their dreams and desires later in life when the opportunities present themselves. This chapter includes spiritual knowledge and wisdom for the development and well-being of you and your child and this is the secret to obtaining success, healing and fulfilment in life. It covers important issues from some of the chapters to help refresh you to the care and nurturing of your psychic child.

The answer is to balance the mind, body and spirit so that they harmonise ,therefore creating a wonderful vibration. If one is out of balance, then the others will be too as they all depend on each other and interpenetrate with one another. It is the vibration that you hold that determines what you attract to you in your daily life and to get the best out of life then you need a fast and light vibration. Your unique vibration is the energy field that resonates around you known as the aura. Below you will read ways in which to raise your vibes so that you can begin to attract the life you desire for you and your child.

Nurturing the Physical Body & Mind

Just as a plant would need good soil, tendering and watering to flourish and grow, so does the physical body need special care and attention! The body consists of around 60 to70% water which is why it is important to keep ourselves hydrated with plenty of filtered water. In his book 'The Miracle of Water' by Dr Masaru Emoto, he covers his research in taking photographs of the crystals that are in the water when positive or negative words and thoughts are spoken over the water. The actual words love and gratitude have an amazing positive effect within the water turning the crystals into the most glorious of sights. As your body is also made up from water then your actual thoughts and feelings will have an affect on your overall health and well-being.

It is therefore important to strive to have good positive thoughts about yourself and towards others as your mind can affect your body. Negative thoughts towards others will still affect you as you are creating them within your mind and this will affect your energy flow. When you send out bad vibes to another, they will also feel them at a subtle energetic level and remember what you give out will also be returned to you , good or bad. Long-term negative thoughts and feelings create a build up of negative energy that can manifest itself as physical and emotional problems with your health, even things such as deep depression. By showing your child that you love and accept yourself for who you are ,then you are creating a great example for them to love and care for themselves also.

Whenever you pour yourself a glass of water from now on, speak the word love over it or ask God to bless the water – I say 'love and light' over any food or drink that I consume as this increases the vibration of the water and food and that is great for my body and well-being.

Obviously, it is also important to eat a balanced diet and whenever possible with meals made from fresh produce and not the microwave kind, as they are far better for you. Yes, we live in a busy world and cooking from scratch is not always possible but fresh food will hold a *lighter vibration* for when it enters out bodies. Food is our fuel that drives our physical body into action and our energy levels can go up and down depending on the type of food we eat. Life- giving foods hold more life -force energy and have a positive affect on our bodies and mind. Any junk food consumed will bring with it a dull vibration offering only short-term satisfaction. Our bodies will soon crave more substance. Whenever possible a good home -cooked family meal is an important part of keeping the family unit bonded together where they can eat and communicate their daily events. This instils family values and friendship and any blessings said over the food before you eat will add to raising the vibration of your meal, which will benefit everyone there.

The body needs movement to keep itself subtle and in good working order. Not only does exercise help with the strength and vitality of the body, it also benefits the state of your mind. Exercising causes the body to produce endorphins, chemicals that help you to feel more peaceful and happy inside. The positive effects of these feelings can also help people who are suffering with depression or having problems with sleep, among many other illnesses. The body and mind are in a state of interpenetrating and lack of physical exercise can limit the body in its full use, which will affect the state of the mind. There are many ways in which you can begin exercising and these can include playing some kind of sport and maybe even being part of a team. It is very encouraging for your child to be part of some team or sport as this can build their confidence and help them to interact with others so they learn how to make friends easily.

The Ego

Our unique personality includes our ego, which is often the driving -force behind our decisions until we learn to use and trust our intuition. Our ego includes beliefs about the way we perceive ourselves, others and the world at large. Do you look on life as if the glass is half-full or half empty? If so this will determine the results you will attract. When we are too egotistical we block out our spiritual side and live life by only acknowledging the fives senses and looking to the material world for fulfilment. An egotistical person can be overpowering, controlling and manipulative as they try to control situations and people around them for their own desires. The ego can also work against you by allowing you to believe that you are no good and therefore you will lack self-belief and confidence within.

You will be out of balance as your ego is holding you back from creating the life of your dreams and desires. In other words it is important to find harmony and balance with our ego so that it will work for us in the best possible way. Do not turn your child into thinking they are so special that they are better than everyone else; this is not only damaging to the child as they will soon fall off their pedestal but you will also be interfering in their spiritual growth. You balance the ego by incorporating the sixth sense and your spiritual side along with the five senses and life in the material world.

Listen to your Heart

Our intuition will manifest itself through the feelings we receive within our heart centre. It is important to honour any emotions and feelings you receive because if they are not acknowledged they can become blocks in your life, creating problems and obstacles. You will also block your spiritual growth by refusing to take responsibility to grow and change. Sometimes too much mental analysing on a problem can cause you to be mentally exhausted and indecisive. By listening to what your heart is telling you, then you are being given the answers needed to make you happy and healthy in your life. To hear the truth in your heart, you need to stay emotionally balanced. In doing so you will find that you do not over- react to life experiences and when you come face to face with any obstacles you are ready to deal with them. To have a balanced emotional state you can use this standpoint of changing what needs to be changed and accepting what can't. This empowers you and gives you the strength to live your life in the present moment, letting go of the past and not worrying about the future before it has even happened. Below are some helpful ways in which to balance your emotions so that you find it easy to listen to what your heart is trying to tell you.

*Positive thinking – when you catch yourself thinking negative thoughts, immediately flip- switch them by reversing the thought to a positive one. Eventually you will retrain your mind. When you clear away the mental blocks you will then make room to hear the feelings of your heart.

*Affirmations – these empower you and you can say them when you are not busy to keep your mind from wandering to anything that will cause your emotional level to drop. A great affirmation is – every day in every way, my confidence is growing stronger and stronger.

*Change your attitude to things – a great spiritual goal should be: do unto others as you would have others do unto you. Focus on the glass is half full and remember an attitude of gratitude will help you to attract more things to be grateful for.

*Remember who you really are – a spiritual being with a Divine spark of God having a human experience. This stops the ego from taking control and making the mistake of focussing only on the self and the material world.

Nurturing your Spirit

Whether you are aware of it or not, the state of your environment has an effect on your overall health. If you live in the city, it is important to have time to connect with nature. When you are walking amongst the greenery and beauty of the countryside or along a beautiful sandy beach, you are cleansing any absorbed negative energy away from your body and mind and you give your spirit a refreshing treat. Your spirit needs to be nurtured and you do this by offering love and service to others and also by honouring your own needs and desires. You will find it easy to connect with your spirit when you take time to mediate or when you connect with nature. You and your child need to go outdoors often even if you don't feel in the mood and you will be surprised by how quickly your moods will lighten. Your spirit will need to feel nurtured and this will help when you are in a place of beautiful energy and good vibes. If you live in an area of negativity and you have no means of moving at this time, there are ways in which you can lighten the vibration of your own living space. This will affect the way you feel and remember it is important to raise your vibes to be able to attract positive things towards you such as a move to somewhere happier. Some ways in which to lighten the vibration of your home are included below –

*Clear away the clutter – a cluttered house is a cluttered

mind.

*Keep everything clean and tidy – cleanliness is next to Godliness – this brings a lighter vibration in your home.

*Include beautiful pictures or ornaments such as pictures of nature, angel ornaments and other high vibrational objects – remember everything holds a vibration and you should remove any negative things from your child's room and yours.

*You can include beautiful crystals around your home – amethyst for protection, rose quartz for healing.

*Include plants and flowers in your home, as these hold life force energy

*Candles and incense are also great ways to bring light and harmony into your living space.

*Books that carry a high level of light will help to increase the overall vibration of your house.

*The power of prayer and inviting the angels to protect your home will also increase the light there.

Parenting a Psychic Child

Sometimes it can be hard for a child to express to their parents what it is they are actually experiencing. If the child is seeing or talking to spirits then they may have trouble in explaining this when telling their Mum or Dad. Parents who are fearful or disbelieve their child's stories can cause more harm than good in how they react to what they hear. If they totally disregard their child's story as make- believe and end up telling their child to stop lying or that they are being silly, then this can cause their little one to become confused. They will start doubting their contact with the spirits and they will also doubt themselves. This confusion can manifest issues of trust in early childhood when the child loses confidence in their creative abilities because they are unsure of their own intuitive nature and tend to listen to what others want for them instead of what they truly want. Take the time to listen to your child and have patience with them even if you are not entirely certain that you believe them.

Parents may be scared or even fearful of what their psychic child is displaying because they have been taught by others to believe that it is evil to communicate with the spirit world. They can then pass on those same ingrained fears to the child if they express them and the child will then believe they must be very bad themselves to have had these psychic experiences. If the child thinks that they are bad, even though they had no control of it, they will automatically create an emotional mental block within them that they will carry throughout their childhood in their subconscious. This emotional and mental block will carry guilt and fear of God because they have been habitually told that it is evil. They may even fear that they will be punished by God for any communication with spirits or ghosts. If you have had this experience as a parent then it is wise to understand that you have only learned these beliefs because they have come from someone else's beliefs. You will have no doubt in your heart that God is a God of unconditional love and with his love you can dissolve your mental and emotional conditioning from your past.

Religious mental conditioning in childhood is a hard lesson to overcome but one that can definitely be overcome through study, meditation and prayer and guidance from God. If you need help to remove this old conditioning because you don't want to pass it on to your child then pray for guidance and know that 'when the student is ready the teacher will appear'. God will send you the right people along your life's path to help guide you along the next phase of your life and heal your past. Reading this book is a nudge from God as you gain insight into the life of a psychic child. In doing so, you also find out more about your spiritual nature. If you were a psychic child yourself and have been brought up with this strict religious mental conditioning from your own parents, then give yourself a break from the guilt and learn to listen to your heart and soul and not the ingrained trappings of the ego.

The Bogey Man

Another issue that parents need to be aware of is what they say to their child when their child is naughty. Telling their child that the 'Bogey Man' will come get them if they are bad, will instil fear of the dark, open closets, the gap under the bed and ghosts or spirits. To them the 'Bogey Man' can be very real as they may have been seeing and talking to spirits for some time and so they imagine that he must be a bad spirit who will come and hurt them. Intimidation and fear as a form of punishing a child for being naughty is not the best way to go if you don't want a child who becomes fearful of trying out new experiences and adventures.

Remember what you teach a child will become their grounding of the way they perceive all future life experiences. We owe it to our little ones to help guide them along their early years with the support and encouragement they deserve. Parents can find positive ways of disciplining their child as this helps the child to learn boundaries as well as learning important life lessons for adulthood. God has entrusted you as parents to guide and teach your children in the best possible way so that they can grow up balanced and happy and be able to accomplish what it is they have come to Earth to do, in other words 'their destiny'.

The most important thing is to let your child know how loved they are. This love offers them a feeling of safety and security and of being wanted. It is also important to pass on spiritual guidance so that they are able to make the best of their lives. When you help to nurture and encourage your child in their early years of development, you are laying down a grounding and manual for them to use when they are older. Children who do not receive this tender care will slowly shut down their feelings and become numb to others in life and therefore block out love from their hearts and ignore their intuitive nature.

Final Thoughts

Let your light shine not only for yourself but also as a beacon of light to your child and those who are still spiritually sleeping. Let your spirit guide you by remembering the power you have within you to create success and healing in your life. Teach your child that they are special and come with the light of God inside them and when the going gets tough they can ask for spiritual guidance and help. Remind them that they have an angel to talk with who will help to protect them from harm. Encourage them to rely on their intuitive nature and honour their feelings to guide them throughout their life. You can do this also for yourself. Know that it is normal for your child to remember things that you may have long forgotten and so give them your patience and love. Finally, I wish you and your children angel blessings throughout your life on earth and for that you can be certain that the angels are already there.

Joanne Brocas

To find out more about Joanne and her work you can visit her website
www.feelthevibes.org

BOOKS

O is a symbol of the world, of oneness and unity. In different cultures it also means the "eye," symbolizing knowledge and insight. We aim to publish books that are accessible, constructive and that challenge accepted opinion, both that of academia and the "moral majority."

Our books are available in all good English language bookstores worldwide. If you don't see the book on the shelves ask the bookstore to order it for you, quoting the ISBN number and title. Alternatively you can order online (all major online retail sites carry our titles) or contact the distributor in the relevant country, listed on the copyright page.

See our website www.o-books.net for a full list of over 500 titles, growing by 100 a year.

And tune in to myspiritradio.com for our book review radio show, hosted by June-Elleni Laine, where you can listen to the authors discussing their books.

mySpiritRadio